Principles of Abilities and Human Learning

Michael J.A. Howe

3/97

UNIVERSITY OF
WOLVERHAMPTON

'002

D0718226

SKS   Psych

UNIVERSITY OF WOLVERHAMPTON
LIBRARY

2222383   CLASS 312

CONTROL   155.
0863775322   4

DATE   SITE
27. OCT. 1998 WV   HOW

WITHDRAWN

Psychology Press

a member of the Taylor & Francis group

Copyright © 1998 by Psychology Press Ltd, a member of the Taylor & Francis group
All rights reserved. No part of this book may be reproduced in any form, by pho-
tostat, microform, retrieval system, or any other means without the prior written
permission of the publisher.

Psychology Press, Publishers
27 Church Road
Hove
East Sussex, BN3 2FA
UK

British Library Cataloguing in Publication Data

A catalogue record for this book is available from the British Library

ISBNs   0-86377-532-2 (Hbk)
         0-86377-533-0 (Pbk)

Cartoons by Rachael Adams.
Cover design by Joyce Chester.
Typeset by Kate Williams, Swansea.
Printed and bound in the United Kingdom by T.J. International Ltd.

Contents

Gaining human abilities

1

This book is about human abilities and the ways in which people acquire and extend them. There are plenty of reasons for wanting to know about abilities, one being that we can make practical use of this knowledge to help add to our own capabilities and attainments. The fact that we can learn is often taken for granted, but a moment's reflection reminds us that there is something quite marvellous about the power that people have to transform themselves by acquiring capabilities in the form of new skills and knowledge. The unique individual each of us becomes is partly created by the learning activities that make a person capable and well informed. The book contains many useful facts about people's learned capabilities and the mental processes that make it possible for individuals to gain them.

Where do abilities come from?

How do our abilities arise? The answer to that question is not immediately obvious. Imagine that you are sitting on a park bench and a spaceship lands in front of you. Out jumps a little space alien. He dances around for a few seconds, sings a song, and finally jumps on a bicycle and disappears back into the spaceship. You find yourself wondering how the alien was *capable* of doing those things. What was needed to make the accomplishments possible? What made the little alien able to do the actions you observed? There are a number of possibilities:

- One is that some kind of internal mechanism governs the activities, just as clockwork dolls are made to move by cogs and levers. The machinery that would be necessary in order for the little alien to carry out the actions you saw would have to be more complicated than that. Yet some impressively complex kinds of behaviour have been observed in living creatures that have brains which are wired-up in advance to act in particular ways. In certain insects, for example, such "pre-wired" brains carry out lengthy sequences of actions.

- A second possible explanation is that the little alien's brain operates like a computer that has been programmed to do the dancing, singing, and bicycling activities you observed. Striking human-like feats are possible when a computer is combined with software that instructs it how to utilise its processing capacities. Perhaps aliens, like computers, are programmed to undertake human-like activities.

However, you are now informed that the little alien is not really an alien after all, but just a human child in fancy dress. Does that discovery influence your efforts to explain the behaviours you saw? It certainly does. It is now clear that neither of the two explanations is correct. You can quickly rule out the first one, that the behaviour was controlled by pre-wired mental mechanisms. The brains of humans, unlike those of insects, are not wired-up in advance to perform complicated activities. This is fortunate for humans, for although it is true that pre-wired brains can do certain things quite well, they also have crippling limitations. The actions of which pre-wired brains are capable are rigid and stereotyped. They have none of the flexibility that allows people to adapt their behaviour to the varying demands of human life.

The second possibility can be eliminated, too. It is true that human brains are similar to computers in some ways, but in other ways they are not like computers at all. In contrast with computers, people cannot extend their capabilities just by inserting into themselves, or "reading in", instructions in the form of software that tells the processing capacities what to do. We may wish that was possible: if only I could just plug a foreign language program into my brain one evening and wake up the next morning speaking fluent French or impeccable Chinese! That many people want to believe that this can be done is demonstrated by the healthy sales of so-called "Subliminal" auditory tapes in Britain and America. The idea is that you listen to a tape, and messages that you are not aware of hearing enter your brain, making you healthier, slimmer, better at remembering, more self-confident, or more attractive to the opposite sex, according to the content of the subliminal information on the tape. There is just one problem with this: it doesn't work, except in the world of science fiction! That way of gaining new abilities is closed to us, because human minds do not work that way. Unlike computers, our brains are not capable of gaining new knowledge and new skills without our making an active effort.

The fact is that we humans are capable of doing things for reasons that are quite unlike the reasons why computers and clockwork dolls can carry out various activities. We have to acquire for ourselves the various kinds of knowledge and skills that make us capable of living successful and independent lives. That acquisition process often involves a degree of active effort and attention, and the process of gaining new capabilities can be a time-consuming one, and sometimes arduous. People undertake various mental activities in order to gain the various kinds of knowledge and skill that humans require. We have a useful shorthand word for these mental activities. The word is learning.

Learning and what it achieves

Learning and human abilities are closely related to each other. The abilities people gain are largely the outcome of their learning activities. Much of the learning that people do contributes to the acquisition and improvement of their abilities.

To return to our little alien, knowing that he was not an alien after all, but a young human being, we can be sure that the capabilities we observed had to be acquired by that individual. They were not built-in like those of a clockwork doll or an insect having a pre-wired brain. Nor were they simply plugged into the child's brain in the way that software is inserted into a computer. Somehow or other the child *learned* them.

Everyone agrees that learning is important, but we do not always appreciate just how heavily each of us depends on our capacity to learn. As well as enabling people to gain all kinds of useful information and everyday skills, ranging from brushing one's teeth to reading a book, learning profoundly influences the ways in which we actually experience our day-to-day lives:

- Our preferences and our likes and dislikes are largely learned.
- So too are our attitudes, interests, and tastes.
- Your sense of humour and my capacity to enjoy a good joke depend on what each of us has learned in the past.

- Learning, or its absence, constrains the kinds of conversations we are capable of having.
- Our choices of movies to see, books to read, and music to listen to, and our preferences when we choose a newspaper or magazine, or select a television channel, are all strongly influenced by our previous learning.

So, as well as equipping us with the knowledge and skills that allow us to get on with our lives, learning plays a big role in forming the kind of individual each person becomes. Differences between people in what they have learned can largely explain why men and women vary so much in the ways in which they perceive and make sense of the events that comprise daily living, and in how they react to many kinds of experiences.

One reason why psychologists study human learning is to gain a better understanding of how human abilities are acquired. Investigations of human learning lead to practical insights that can be applied in order to help make people more effective learners. In this book we shall discover how learning makes it possible for individuals to acquire some of the skills a person needs. We also explore the ways in which people gain the various kinds of knowledge and information that help someone to become a competent adult.

Learning takes many different forms, but common to all of them is the fact that they involve the person becoming altered in some way, thereby gaining new abilities or extending old ones. In forming new abilities, two broad categories of learned changes are particularly crucial:

- First, much learning involves a person gaining some or other kind of *knowledge*. Broadly speaking, a person's knowledge, which is often based on language, takes the form of the various items of information and other things the individual *knows* about. People extend their knowledge as an outcome of attending to items of information that are unfamiliar but nevertheless understandable.
- Second, as a result of learning, various mental and physical *skills* are acquired. In contrast with knowledge, many skills are unrelated to language. They take the form of actions that a person can *do*. Skills are often gained by doing an activity or by practising. Sometimes this involves imitating the skills of another person.

In practice, many of the attainments and accomplishments that people acquire through learning involve combinations of both knowledge and skills. Human abilities often involve knowledge and skills combined. Many of the most important practical questions about human psychology revolve around the ways in which learning provides people with useful knowledge and skills. Here are just a few examples. These are some of the questions that have prompted the writing of this book:

How are mental and physical skills gained?
What does it mean to have expertise?
How are people's abilities related to their intelligence levels?
Why and how do people differ in what they can do?

How important is early learning, and what are its long-term effects?
In what ways do a person's abilities depend on family background?
How can parents help their children to learn?

How does existing knowledge affect new learning and remembering?

How effective is memory training?
Do skills transfer?
What study skills are most effective?

How do children gain general-purpose strategies for
learning?
How does motivation influence abilities?
How do people become successful at physical skills?
In what ways do personality and temperament affect
learning?

How and why do certain people become geniuses?
What are the advantages and disadvantages of specialising?
What are child prodigies?

There are plenty of reasons for wanting to be able to answer questions like these. There is no guarantee that reading this book will make you an expert on all these matters, but it will make you well equipped to give informed answers.

How this book is arranged

We can think of the mental machinery that makes it possible for people to learn as being not unlike a kind of manufacturing process. It is a process that enables individuals to forge ahead and extend their capabilities by adding to their knowledge and skills. In the present chapter a main goal will be to begin to understand how the learning process actually works.

We start by enquiring into the kinds of events that create learning or help make it possible. We ask, "What has to happen in order for learning to take place?" Also, "When and why does learning occur?" Research studies have revealed some important facts about the ways in which we humans acquire our capabilities. Some of the findings of research into human learning will be described in the remainder of this chapter. We shall discover that it is possible to extract some important general *principles* of human learning.

Chapter 2 examines some of the abilities that people gain in their early years. Young children acquire a number of basic capacities that they can draw on throughout life. These include language, reading, numerical abilities, and various physical skills. The chapter considers the question of whether it is possible and desirable to accelerate early considerably more accurate when people have been encouraged to take an active part in the learning process.

We can note in passing that the children's retention of new information in the experiments I have described could just as readily be described as being an instance of *remembering* as an example of *learning*. As it happens, in situations where the learner's aim is to gain new information or add to their store of knowledge, the words "learning" and "remembering" are often interchangeable. Saying "She learned the poem" has roughly the same meaning as "She memorised the poem": only the words are different. Of course, in *some* circumstances there are important differences in what we mean by the words learning and remembering, but because they are overlapping terms there is usually no reason to be too concerned about making a distinction between them. It is helpful think of the word "learning" as a broad term that refers not just to one kind of activity, but to a whole family of processes and mental events that, in one way or another, allows people to add to their knowledge or increase their skills and capabilities.

We have discovered something useful from the experiment I described, which can be expressed as a simple basic rule or principle of learning, as follows:

Learning takes place as the result of active mental processing.

This is only a start, but it is a good start. The rule serves to emphasise that people do not learn by passively absorbing information, and that it is important to actively concentrate on the task. The chances are that you will have encountered a number of practical ways for improving your effectiveness as a learner by making the task of studying an active one, rather than one in which information is passively absorbed. For example:

1. Many people find that when reading in order to add to knowledge it is helpful to underline important words. Research findings have confirmed that doing this can have a positive effect.
2. Again, when you are studying, an effective strategy is to try to express the information you are reading in your own words. Doing this is especially effective when the material is somewhat unfamiliar or difficult.
3. In addition, simply writing down words and ideas can be helpful. This is partly because it is useful to make a record of important information. Also, the actual activity of writing can

abilities. It also investigates the effectiveness of learning programmes that are intended to compensate children for the ill-effects of early deprivation.

Chapter 3 raises a number of questions about the actual nature of abilities. What exactly *are* abilities? What are they like? What are their most important characteristics? How can different capabilities and different items of knowledge become joined to one another? In what circumstances does something learned in one situation transfer to new or different tasks, or become applicable to new challenges? What is the relationship between specific abilities and general intelligence? The answers to some of these questions are surprisingly different from what common sense might lead us to expect.

Chapter 4 starts with the fact that because the necessary mental activities that produce learning demand a certain amount of time and effort, a person has to have good reasons for engaging in them. One way of expressing this is by saying that for the manufacturing of learning to take place there needs to be some kind of fuel to make the process work. The fuel for human learning is provided by *motivation*. This supplies a person with the reason or incentive for doing whatever is necessary in order to make learning happen, making it possible for abilities to be gained. There are negative as well as positive motivational influences, but motivation drives people's efforts to learn. Chapter 4 investigates how that occurs.

The abilities that were examined in Chapter 2 provide a foundation on which it is possible to build more advanced human accomplishments. Some of these abilities are surveyed in Chapter 5, which investigates relatively complex and difficult attainments. This chapter examines the effects of practise on various capabilities. It considers ways in which individuals gain expertise at various accomplishments. The use of memory aids and learning techniques is examined. The circumstances in which people gain exceptionally high levels of ability are also investigated. Other topics examined in this chapter include the influence of intelligence, the possible roles of innate gifts and talents, and the significance of regarding certain individuals as being child prodigies and geniuses.

The best way to test the value of whatever we discover about learning and the acquisition of abilities is to see if we can use it to help ourselves extend our own capacities. Does this knowledge work for us? Can we make use of it in our everyday lives? So Chapter 6 turns the camera on ourselves. The intention here is to apply to our own activities some of the findings and insights that were encountered in the earlier chapters. Chapter 6 specifically addresses the question of how to learn and study more effectively. It examines ways of improving the effectiveness of learning activities based on reading. The chapter also provides advice on improving writing skills and on studying for exams. The aim here is to help you, the reader, to improve your effectiveness at acquiring needed capabilities.

Principles of learning: 1. Active mental processing

What has to happen in order for a person to learn? Without more ado we shall take a closer look at some of the ways in which people add to their knowledge and skills. We shall attempt to extract some basic general principles of human learning. We start with a description of an experiment conducted by psychologists who were investigating how young children augment their knowledge (Turnure, Buium, & Thurlow, 1976). The study explored some of the influences that affect the likelihood of young children retaining information they have been given. The aim of the experiment was to discover which of a number of different mental activities was most effective for promoting this kind of learning.

All the children who participated in the study were shown illustrations of common objects that were already familiar to them, such as a shoe or a carrot. In one condition of the experiment children were simply told to say what the objects were. Two items were displayed at a time, and each child was shown 21 pairs of objects. Afterwards, each child was shown just one of the objects from each pair, and asked if he or she could remember what other item had been paired with it.

These children recalled very little of the information. Five-year-olds, for example, could remember on average only one item out of the 21. Clearly, just looking at items is not an effective procedure for helping a learner to remember them. Although that is a procedure that works well with computers, which are good at storing information that has been "read" into them, it is not nearly so effective with humans, as this finding demonstrates. It is clear that something else has to happen if a more substantial amount of the information to which children are exposed is to be retained by them, so that it can be recalled when they need it.

What else must occur? A hint of a possible answer is provided by the old saying that learning is an active rather than a passive process. Does it help if the learner plays a more active role? Of course, a person who is merely attending to some information that is being displayed is being more active than someone who is not attending to it at all. But as we have just seen, simply attending, on its own, does not seem to be enough to guarantee learning. So it would be interesting to see what happens when people who are presented with information are encouraged to deal with it in a considerably more active manner.

In the Turnure et al. (1976) study, this was made to happen by getting some of the child participants to carry out various kinds of mental activities in relation to the illustrations that were shown to them. In one of the conditions of the experiment the children were told to make up a sentence that joined together the two objects shown in the illustrations. For example, if one illustration showed a bar of soap and the picture that was paired with it depicted a shoe, an appropriate linking sentence would be "The soap is hiding in the shoe". In another experimental condition children were once again encouraged to be mentally active, but this time their activity took the form of answering a question about the pictured objects rather than making up a linking sentence. The children who participated in this condition were given questions that encouraged them to think about the possible relationships of the two objects shown in the illustrations. For example, when the pictures depicted a shoe and a bar of soap, the question might be "What is the soap doing under the shoe?", or "Why is the soap in the shoe?".

The researchers discovered that having to carry out mental activities led to substantial increases in the number of objects the children were able to remember. Those children who made up sentences joining the objects retained eight items out of the 21, on average. The children who answered questions about the objects did even better than that: for them, the average number of items correctly recalled was 16 out of the 21. In short, those children who were encouraged to deal with the new information in a manner that was more active than merely identifying the objects they saw retained much more information than the other children. They recalled up to sixteen times as many of the objects they had been shown.

This finding demonstrates an important principle, namely that a learning session can be made very much more effective simply by encouraging individuals to take a more active stance. Essentially the same finding has been observed in numerous other studies. There is a clear practical implication here: if you want to maximise learning, make sure that the individual takes an active approach to the learning process. It is not just children who benefit from being instructed to take an active role in the learning process. Studies have shown that in adults, too, the retention of information over a lengthy period of time is

aid learning, as has been established by researchers investigating the effectiveness of note-taking.

Principles of learning: 2. Making meaningful connections

In practice, mental activity is just one side of a coin. There are various reasons why active mental processing is effective. An especially important one is that it has the effect of either forming links within the information being learned, or making connections between the material to be learned and information that is already familiar to the learner, or both of these.

This connection-forming outcome of taking an active approach to learning makes a big difference. It aids learning by transforming the task from one of retaining a large number of unrelated small items — something that for human learners is very difficult — to one that most people find much easier, that of retaining a smaller number of larger items. Because the process of forming connections makes a large contribution to learning, it provides the kernel of a second rule or principle of learning. This states that:

> *Human abilities are extended as a result of mental processing that involves perceiving meaningful connections between new information and the learner's existing knowledge.*

A typical instance of this general statement is the fact that people find it easier to learn new facts when they can connect them to something they already know. New information that is totally unconnected to anything at all familiar is often confusing. It can be very difficult to understand, and impossible to learn except by the slow and inefficient process of learning by rote. Finding connections between new information and existing knowledge overcomes this problem.

As is the case with the first principle, the truth of the second one has been demonstrated in numerous psychological experiments. In one study, for instance, adult learners were told to listen carefully to some simple sentences such as the following ones:

The bald man read the newspaper
The funny man bought a ring

Later, they were asked various questions designed to test how much of the information had been retained (Bransford, Stein, Shelton, & Owings, 1981). Their scores on the memory test were unremarkable, with about four out of ten questions being correctly answered, on average.

Another group of participants in the experiment listened to sentences that were considerably longer. For these people, instead of the short sentences, they heard:

> The bald man read the newspaper to look for a hat sale
> The funny man bought a ring that squirted water

Note that these sentences contained more information than the shorter ones, so the listeners might have been expected to retain a smaller proportion of the information in them. However, the reverse happened. Participants provided the correct answers to questions such as "Which man read the newspaper?" on seven occasions out of ten.

This finding may seem rather odd. Why should providing a larger amount of information make the task of retaining it easier rather than more difficult? The answer is fairly simple. With the longer sentences,

but not the shorter ones, it was possible for participants to form connections, by making use of what they already knew to discern meaningful links in the information. With a sentence like "The funny man bought a ring", it is true that there are essentially only two propositions to be retained. These are, first, that the man was funny, and, second, that he bought a ring. But they are entirely *separate* facts, with no non-arbitrary connection or relationship between them. With "The funny man bought a ring that squirted water", however, although it is true that there are as many as three propositions (the two previous ones plus the fact that the ring squirted water) they can now be seen to be interconnected, provided that the learner already possesses the knowledge of a link between funniness and rings that squirt water. For such a learner, it is not necessary to retain three separate propositions, because the links join them together into one. It is this that makes the task of retaining the information easier.

Generally speaking, we humans are not good at retaining large numbers of unrelated facts. We do much better when, by making use of knowledge we already possess, we can connect the facts together. Whenever this can be done the separate elements come together in a kind of chain. Consequently, when we are trying to learn or remember them, one item leads us to the next one.

A further experiment provides a neat demonstration of this. In that study, subjects were asked to concentrate on lists containing 10 unrelated nouns for a minute and then try to recall the words (Bower & Clark, 1969). There were 12 lists in all. These tasks caused little difficulty, and the majority of the participants remembered most of the items correctly. However, after all 12 lists had been inspected and recalled, subjects in the experiment were asked to write down as many as possible of all the 120 words that had appeared in the 12 lists. This was a far more difficult challenge for the subjects. At this stage most of them recalled less than 20% of the total number of words.

However, some of the participants, who had inspected the same lists as the other participants, and for the same amount of time, had been given special instructions. These instructions encouraged them to form connections between the words in the lists. These people had been told not just to concentrate on each of the lists presented to them, but to try to make up a sentence that joined together the words in that list. For example, with a word list such as:

VEGETABLE   INSTRUMENT   COLLEGE   NAIL   FENCE
BASIN   MERCHANT   QUEEN   SCALE   GOAT

a possible sentence might be,

A VEGETABLE can be a useful INSTRUMENT for a COLLEGE student: a carrot can be a NAIL for your FENCE or BASIN, but a MERCHANT of the QUEEN would SCALE that fence and feed the carrot to a GOAT

After a few trial attempts, these participants found it quite easy to make up appropriate sentences. Doing this had a dramatic and positive impact on learning. The effects were not apparent in the earlier stage of the experiment, because even those participants who did not make connecting sentences performed well when they were first asked to recall each list of words, immediately after it had been inspected. At that early stage of the experiment there had been little room for improvement.

At the later stage, however, when subjects were asked to recall all the words they could remember from all 10 lists, those individuals who had been told to form connecting sentences from the words in each list were much more successful than the other subjects. In contrast with the others, who could remember only around 20% of all the words, these participants recalled around 90%. That is, at the end of the experiment, those subjects who had been told to connect the word items to each other recalled more than four times as many words as the other subjects did.

These link-making activities assist learning by making connections *within* material that is to be learned. In everyday life it can be equally helpful to make links *between* the new information and the learner's existing knowledge. The latter kind of links predominate when the information being learned is highly meaningful. In particular, when someone is trying to learn something that is unfamiliar, it is often helpful for teachers to provide students with material that forms such links by functioning as an *advance organiser* (Ausubel, 1968). The term refers to information that bridges any gaps between the new material and the learner's existing knowledge, thereby making it easier for the learner to connect the information that is to be learned with what they already know.

For example, when teaching a student about a new and unfamiliar method of life-saving, it could be helpful to start by drawing the student's attention to a method that is already familiar, and then point out ways in which the new method is similar to the familiar one and ways in which it is different. Providing an advance organiser like this would make it easier for the learner to make use of existing knowledge to form connections that would assist learning of the new and unfamiliar material.

We regularly encounter advance organisers in a very simple form whenever *metaphors* are introduced in order to communicate abstract or new ideas. Essentially, metaphors aid communication by transforming information into a more familiar and concrete form. So when we talk about an idea *dying off*, or a theory being *half-baked* or being *buttressed* with firm evidence, we understand what is being said. This is because the ideas being expressed are readily connected to our existing knowledge, because they are expressed in words that are already clear and familiar.

Principles of learning: 3. Repetition

The final of our three principles of learning simply states that:

Repetition aids learning.

In practice, it is useful to make a distinction between different kinds of repetition. First, there are ones that help learners acquire knowledge. Second, there are forms of repetition that assist people in gaining skills.

Rehearsal

To aid knowledge acquisition, the most familiar kind of repetition is rehearsal. Up to a point, most mature learners are aware of the benefits to be gained by rehearsing. All the same, it quite often happens that learners — children especially — handicap themselves by failing to rehearse at times when doing so would be helpful. Or they may restrict their success by adopting a less than effective rehearsal strategy.

The benefits of repetition in the form of rehearsal activities are particularly apparent when young learners who do not normally rehearse are encouraged to do so. If children are presented with the kind of learning task in which rehearsal would be beneficial, some individuals as young as 5 years of age will rehearse, and by the age of about 10 the majority will do so.

Fortunately for researchers investigating the benefits of rehearsing, with young children it is relatively easy to know whether they are rehearsing or not, because most of them move their lips when doing so. In one study it was found that when children were looking at common objects that they had been asked to remember, the oldest children (aged around 10) were more likely to rehearse than the youngest ones (aged 5). It was also found that the older children correctly recalled more items than the young children. At each age, those children who did rehearse recalled more items than those children who did not (Flavell, Beach, & Chinsky, 1966).

These findings are consistent with the suggestion that rehearsal aids learning, but they do not prove that to be the case. It is possible, for example, that older children happen to rehearse more and also just happen to remember, but without the increased rehearsing actually contributing to the improved remembering. However, the findings of a further experiment confirmed that there is indeed a cause-and-effect relationship between rehearsing and learning.

This further step involved selecting some of the children in the previous experiment who did *not* rehearse. These children were shown how to do so, and the effects were observed. It proved quite easy to teach rehearsing to children aged 6 and 7 who initially did not rehearse. This was achieved by simply telling them to whisper the names of objects they were looking at until the time when they are asked to start recalling. Did the children's task performance improve when they followed these instructions? It did indeed, to the extent that they were now recalling as many items as did those children who had spontaneously been using a rehearsal strategy, without needing to be instructed to do so.

This rehearsal experiment shows that young children can readily acquire a strategy of rehearsing, and that doing so considerably augments their ability to learn. The finding has a clear practical implication. It suggests that, especially where school learning is concerned, many young students would gain from their teacher's making sure that they know how to rehearse and encouraging them to do so whenever appropriate.

In practice, however, things are more complicated. That is partly because simply knowing how to rehearse is not enough to ensure that a child will actually do so whenever it is potentially helpful. In order for rehearsal to be done routinely, it is necessary for children to get into the habit of doing so. And for this to happen there may need to be considerable support and encouragement from a teacher or a parent. Eventually, however, a rehearsing habit will become established, and the child will rehearse more or less automatically. When that happens, the improved learning that rehearsing makes possible will follow.

Of course, the effectiveness of repetition and rehearsal will depend on the precise way in which they are carried out, and on the appropriateness of those activities to the particular task. Generally speaking, repetition is likely to be most effective when it accompanies a learning task that an individual finds quite difficult. On the whole, the more difficult the task, the more helpful it is to devote a substantial proportion of the available study time to rehearsal.

This is demonstrated by the findings of a study conducted many years ago (Gates, 1917) in which students of varying ages were told to read a number of short biographies. Afterwards, their knowledge was tested. It was found that at all ages more learning took place when a substantial portion of the study time was spent rehearsing than when the students had simply read the information. Generally speaking, the greatest amount of learning occurred when as much as 50 or 60% of the study time had been devoted to rehearsing. This improved learning by about a third, compared with an approach to study in which students simply read the biographies, and did not rehearse at all. The advantage produced by rehearsing was largest for the youngest children in the study, who were aged around 9 years. For the oldest individuals, who were aged 14, the advantage was smaller.

Repetition and rehearsal can be especially effective when they take the form of activities in which learners test themselves at recalling information they are studying. The effectiveness of such testing is demonstrated by the findings of an experiment in which adolescent students read to themselves a passage containing 12 paragraphs on British history (Duchastel, 1982). It was found that, compared with other learners, students whose recall of the passage was tested immediately after they had finished reading it retained the information over a two-week period far more successfully. Two weeks after the learning session, these students could remember twice as many of the items in the passage as students who had not previously been tested.

Practice

So far, the studies of repetition and practice that have been mentioned are ones that are concerned with the acquisition of knowledge. Repetition also contributes to the learning of skills. In this case the kinds of repetitions that are especially effective involve active practice of a skill rather than verbal rehearsal alone.

Photo courtesy TRIP, photographer J. Okwesa

Repetition in the form of practice is a major component of success at all skills, ranging from those that have a large physical element, such as sporting skills and musical performing skills to those that are primarily intellectual, such as arithmetic and chess-playing. Practice on its own does not always bring success, however. In order to be effective it is important that the particular kind of practice activity that is undertaken is well fitted to the learning task and appropriate to the stage of progress already reached by the individual learner. It is also necessary that the practice task is given all the learner's attention. All the same, practising is immensely important. The amount of effective practice that is undertaken is one of the best predictors (often *the* best single predictor) of the levels of achievement people reach in a wide range of activities.

The sheer amount of practice needed in order to reach really high levels of accomplishment at valued skills may seem dauntingly high. For example, young performing musicians who reach professional standards of expertise will often have devoted as much as 10,000 hours to practising: this constitutes a substantial proportion of a person's time in middle and late childhood. Even to be a good amateur performer, and reach Grade Eight standard of the musical board examinations, takes a young player around 3500 hours of practice, on average.

As we shall demonstrate later, to achieve the highest standards of performance at a difficult skill, *everyone* has to do plenty of practising. The idea that there are a few fortunate individuals who can leap ahead at sports such as football or tennis, or performing skills such as playing the violin, without having to devote long hours to practice, is simply a myth.

Summary

Human abilities are acquired through learning, and this normally involves conscious effort. Learning plays a large role in making people the individual adults they become, as well as equipping people with the skills and abilities they require. As an outcome of engaging in learning activities we gain various kinds of skills, and we also acquire useful knowledge.

In relation to the circumstances in which people extend their abilities by gaining knowledge and skills, research has identified the following three broad principles, all of which are crucial:

- First, learning takes place as the outcome of active mental processing. This has been demonstrated in a number of investigations. A practical implication is that students can maximise their success by ensuring that their role in the learning process is an active one.
- Second, human abilities are gained and extended as a result of learning that involves perceiving meaningful connections between new information and the learner's existing knowledge. People find it easier to learn new facts when they can connect them to something they already know.
- The third broad principle is that repetition aids learning. Repetition can take the form of various activities, including rehearsal (and self-testing) and practising. These make important contributions to the acquisition of abilities.

Further reading

A more detailed account of the contribution of mental processes to learning is provided in J.R. Anderson (1995), *Cognitive psychology and its implications* (New York: Freeman). The contribution of learners' existing knowledge to learning and understanding is discussed in M.J.A. Howe (1985), *A teacher's guide to the psychology of learning* (Oxford: Blackwell).

How children gain basic capabilities 2

B abies start learning in their first months, but newborns arrive in the world already equipped with certain capabilities in the form of "built-in" instinctive behaviours. They include simple reflexes, such as the sucking reflex. These "pre-installed" capacities to act help the baby to survive, especially in the early months before there has been time to gain capabilities through learning.

Some of the capacities that human infants already possess at birth are ones that will help them to make use of opportunities to learn. For example, they can see patterns, they have a preference for human faces over other objects and can distinguish between different facial expressions, and they can move their heads in response to sounds. Even in the first week of life babies can distinguish their mother's voice.

On the whole, as a baby builds up a repertoire of learned abilities, simple reflexes and instincts become less important. However, some of those capabilities that are largely acquired or learned retain substantial innate elements. For example, language depends on learning, but it also depends on the fact that our brains are innately organised in ways that make it possible for language learning to take place quickly and efficiently.

The beginnings of learning

At first sight, a young baby may not appear to be an active learner. However, if you watch a hungry month-old infant who is crying, you may notice that the cries begin to stop just before his mother picks him up to feed him, and before the feeding actually takes place. If instead of picking the child up, the mother stops and starts to walk, the cries will resume. This suggests that the baby has somehow come to know that the mother's

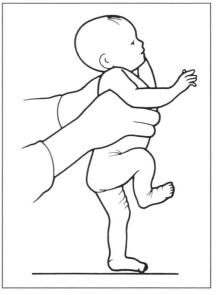

Stepping reflex in newborn baby. Reproduced by permission from *Principles of Development Psychology*, edited by G. Butterworth and M. Harris. © 1994 Lawrence Erlbaum Associates Ltd, Hove, UK.

approach means dinner is on its way. How did that happen? The infant was not born knowing that. Clearly, some learning must have already taken place: the child has started to associate the mother's arrival with imminent feeding.

Another young baby may react differently, but still provide evidence of having acquired, through learning, capacities that were not present at birth. For example, a second child also cries when hungry, but does not cease crying before she is picked up, or even immediately afterwards. Yet that child stops crying as soon as her mother carries her into the room where she is normally fed. If that baby is then taken out of the room she starts to cry again. So it appears that this child too has learned to make a connection. In her case the link she has learned is between feeding and being in a particular room.

With both these babies it is clear that they are already beginning to learn. Also, learning is making a real contribution to their lives. At first, their world would have appeared to them as a confusing and unpredictable succession of random happenings. But as soon as they begin to learn, and start to make connections between various events that happen, babies become capable of perceiving some elements of order and pattern in their everyday world. They become increasingly able to see that daily life is not quite so unpredictable any more. As a consequence of learning, events are no longer so random and confusing as they would have seemed to the infants before they started to make associations between things.

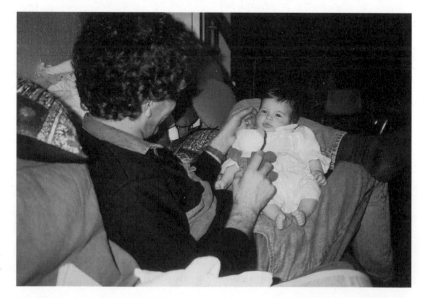

Photo courtesy
TRIP, photographer
H. Rogers

Varieties of infant learning

Prior to language being acquired, the kinds of learning that are possible for young humans are relatively restricted. Some of the forms of early learning that are seen in babies are not entirely unlike the kinds of learning that can be observed in non-human species. For example:

Classical conditioning. In classical conditioning a connection of association is learned, so that a response that was initially elicited by one event is now also elicited by an event that has been paired with the original one. In a dog, for instance, as Ivan Pavlov first demonstrated many years ago, if a buzzer sounds at the same time as food is presented, after a number of pairings of food and buzzer, the response of salivating—which was initially observed only on presentation of the food—is found to occur when the buzzer sounds on its own. Similarly, in a newborn human baby, if she hears the same sound each time she starts receiving milk, the sucking response that was produced by the milk is eventually elicited by the sound on its own, even when no milk is provided.

Operant conditioning. In operant conditioning in animals, responses that are reliably rewarded start to be made at a higher rate. This also happens in human babies. For instance, even in the first week of life babies can learn to vary their rate of sucking in order to gain the reward of hearing their mother's voice. If the sound of the mother's voice is made available whenever the rate of sucking increases, the infant will suck more quickly. If the arrangements are reversed, so that slower rather than faster sucking produces the mother's voice, the speed of sucking will decrease.

Habituation. It is obviously valuable for a person or an animal to be able to react to important events, but it is not possible in practice to respond to every single stimulus. So it is useful to be able to react selectively to new or unexpected events, because they are the ones that are especially likely to be important. Habituation is a kind of learning phenomenon that makes this possible. It occurs in newborns, and even in prenatal infants. What happens with habituation is that whereas the first presentation of a new stimulus elicits a response, the more the stimulus is repeated the less likely it is to produce a reaction.

An experiment involving presenting unfamiliar smells to two-day-olds provides an illustration of habituation in infants. The procedure involved placing a cotton swab containing an odorous solution next to a baby's face for a 10-second period (Engen, Lipsitt, & Kaye, 1963). At first this reliably produced a response by the infant in the form of increased physical activity. However, after presenting an odour on 10 occasions, reactions to it largely ceased. That demonstrated that the baby had habituated to the odour. It was clear that the learning which had taken place was habituation to that particular odour rather than a diminished reaction to new smells in general, because if a different odour was presented, the baby once again made a strong physical response, demonstrating what is called "dishabituation".

Imitative learning. Very young infants are capable of primitive imitative responses, which are gradually replaced by acquired imitation skills. Imitating parents and others is an activity that helps to extend the young child's repertoire of acquired skills.

Armed with the capacity to learn, babies soon begin to make discoveries about the world they inhabit. As early as the first week they may use their mouths to explore new objects. They soon learn to explore hard and soft items differently and make connections between voices and faces. By around four months babies are beginning to have some control over their own lives. They start to be able to make things happen, displaying real pleasure when they do so, for example by knocking a toy down or moving it, or making a noise.

Innate imitation in babies. Reprinted by permission from A.N. Meltzoff and M.K. Moore *Science*, 1977, *198*, 75–8. Copyright 1977 American Association for the Advancement of Science.

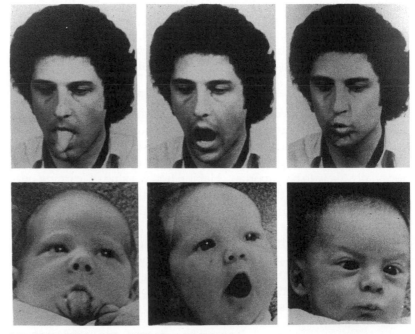

Language

Of all abilities language is the most distinctly human, setting us apart from other species. Its most obvious function is to enable people to communicate with others. However, language is just as essential for making possible the *internal* communications that take place within ourselves. These allow a person to think and reason, to remember events in the past, and make plans for the future.

The work of Noam Chomsky and other scholars has established that the brains we humans inherit are in some respects innately prepared for acquiring language. That is why human children, unlike all other animals, are able to gain the immense amount of information that is needed in order to "know" their own language. Human brains are not simply bigger or more powerful than those of other species, but are also equipped at birth in ways that help to make rapid language learning possible.

Even though babies' brains are in some respects pre-prepared to acquire language, in the infant's first year it is necessary to gain some essential communication skills on which language can build. These can be regarded as "pre-linguistic" or pre-language abilities. For example:

- Babies have to learn how to make the sounds that are used in language.
- They have to learn that sounds can represent objects, events, and experiences.
- They need to learn that the effective use of language involves two individuals taking turns to communicate and attend to the other person.

So a number of pre-language abilities have to be gained. These prepare the young child for acquiring language as such. In most families this preliminary learning takes place informally, as parents play with their babies, talk and sing to them, and engage in games that incorporate language and the activity of communicating with another person. Such activities typically begin well before the baby shows any sign of being able to actually produce words, or even understand them.

The majority of children begin speaking in the early part of their second year. Babies make better progress at language if their parents have encouraged them to gain the basic skills on which language builds. Such parents take an active role in encouraging their children to practise the communication skills that prepare a young person for gaining language.

The earliest form of interpersonal expression. A 6-week-old girl smiles at her mother's face, then responds to gentle baby-talk with cooing vocalisation and a conspicuous hand movement. In the third picture, the mother is imitating the preceding vocalisation of her baby. From *The Social Foundations of Language and Thought*: *Essays in Honor of Jerome J. Bruner* by David R. Olson, editor. © 1980 by David R. Olson. Reprinted by permission of W.W. Norton, New York.

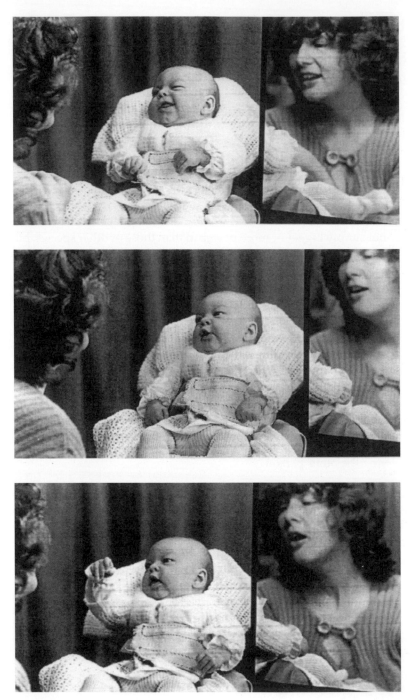

Young children are also helped by having parents who are responsive to a child's early steps towards acquiring language itself. Yet because of the fact that young human brains are innately prepared for learning language, even those young people whose parents do relatively little to actively encourage language acquisition are able to acquire some language skills. Their language development may be delayed and their language skills are likely to be restricted, but only when the deprivation of early experiences is very severe does language acquisition fail to take place at all.

Young children thrive in an environment that is rich in language. This does not mean that each and any kind of exposure to language will help a young child. The sheer amount of talk that a child is exposed to is relatively unimportant, for example. And deliberate language training by parents is not always helpful: in some circumstances it can even have a negative effect on a child's progress. For example, in one investigation it was discovered that children who were rewarded by their mothers for pronouncing words correctly and punished for poor pronunciation actually progressed slower rather than faster than children whose mothers were unconcerned about correct pronunciation (Nelson, Carskaddon, & Bonvallion, 1973).

What *is* helpful however, is for the young child to experience language that is directed towards the child. When parents make an effort to talk to their baby, and encourage and respond to a child's own language, being careful to avoid any criticism and keeping the language activities informal and spontaneous, the child's progress tends to be especially rapid and successful.

The kinds of encouragement that are especially effective for stimulating language learning depend on the stage of progress that has been reached. But at most ages parents can help by asking questions, talking about the child's own activities, acknowledging, imitating, or repeating what the child has said, and providing opportunities for language learning by talking about topics relating to the child's needs and giving careful attention to the child's own attempts to communicate. It is especially helpful when adults talk about an activity that is already engaging the child's attention or an interest that the child is already thinking about.

Accelerating language acquisition

Does language encouragement have long-term effects on children's progress? There is plenty of evidence demonstrating that it does. Children whose parents make an effort to talk to them gain key language skills earlier than other children, and have a far better grasp of language (Hart & Risley, 1995). It is especially helpful for parents to:

- give their children plenty of attention;
- respond to them in ways that are sensitive and encouraging;
- talk to them frequently;
- make an effort to include their children in the parents' own lives.

However, it has been pointed out that the fact that there is a relationship between parental encouragement and children's progress does not in itself provide firm evidence of a cause-and-effect linkage. It is conceivable, for instance, that the relationship between good parenting and good language learning is simply a reflection of genetic causation, i.e. the children of conscientious parents do well just because they share their parents' genes.

Of course, the fact that inherited factors probably make a contribution to the relationship between parenting and progress does not make it less likely that the encouragement and language stimulation given by the parents *also* makes a contribution. But it is necessary to confirm that this is the case: it cannot just be taken for granted. In fact, there now exists a substantial body of research findings establishing that, especially with regard to important aspects of language competence such as gaining a large vocabulary of words, the ways in which parents act towards their children can indeed have a large positive influence on a child's progress at language.

In one investigation (Fowler et al., 1993) the parents of a number of babies were shown how to increase the language-related activities they normally engaged in when playing with their child. At a later stage the long-term consequences were assessed. There was nothing especially novel about the language activities of the parents in Fowler's programme: these mainly took the form of parent-and-child games that were similar to ones that many parents introduce spontaneously. The parents in the study were simply encouraged to alter their ordinary interactions with their babies in four straightforward ways:

- First, they were simply encouraged to introduce language activities more frequently and regularly than they would have done normally, a consequence being that language-based interactions with their children took up a larger amount of time.
- Second, the parents were shown how to introduce different kinds of activities in a manner that was systematically gradu-

ated to take account of the child's stage of development. They were given advice about appropriate language activities. These started with ones involving single word names for objects and actions. They gradually progressed to language activities involving more complex parts of speech and grammatical forms. To help them achieve their aims, the parents were given picture books and lists of words, as well as a training manual.

- Third, the parents were required to keep careful records of their children's progress.
- Fourth, the parents were instructed to begin engaging in language games and activities at an earlier stage in their baby's life than they otherwise would have done.

To assess the effectiveness of Fowler's language programme, the children were tested on a number of occasions. The interventions proved to be extremely effective. For instance, by the age of 1, four of the participating infants were speaking in sentences, a feat that is not normally possible until around 20 months. Also, the use of five-word sentences, which is not usually encountered until around 32 months, was observed in three of the participating infants by 20 months and in the remainder by 24 months. In addition, on various other indications of a child's progress at language, such as using ordinary or self-referral pronouns, and the plural form of nouns, the performance of the children in the study was between five and ten months ahead of the average ages at which these benchmarks are reached. The same was found when the children's scores at a standard language test (the Griffiths Test) was compared with the average scores of children of the equivalent ages.

The participating children's progress was also compared with that of children in a control group, who had received no special treatment. These children's rate of progress was no better than average, and lagged well behind that of the trained children. And the positive effects of the special training were not just temporary. The final occasion on which the children in the study were tested was when they were 5 years old. At this time it was found that the advantages gained by the children who had received special training were still being maintained.

Some additional evidence of the effectiveness of the activities introduced by the parents in Fowler's study was provided by examining the progress of one child in the study whose mother decided to discontinue the special training when he was 1 year old. When the child was tested six months later it was found that his language score, in contrast with the scores of the other participants, had dropped by over 30 points. His IQ score had also decreased substantially.

The success of Fowler's investigation provides strong evidence that giving children extra encouragement to gain language can make a real difference. However, it is clear that the intervention was quite intensive, involving a fair amount of time and effort on the part of the parents. Does this mean that language acquisition can only be accelerated by intervention programmes that are intensive and of long duration? Not necessarily: the findings of another research investigation indicate that even relatively brief interventions may be highly effective. A study conducted by Grover Whitehurst and his colleagues (Whitehurst et al., 1988) showed that substantial and long-lasting advantages can be produced by a shorter and less intensive programme of language activities.

Whitehurst's investigation concentrated on training parents to give their children special help during the times when the parents were reading stories to their young children, aged between 21 months and 35 months. One group of parents were given instructions about activities to engage in during these times. There was also a control group, comprising children whose parents spent an equivalent amount of time reading to them, but these parents were not given special training or instructions.

The participating parents were taught to encourage their children to make active use of language during the daily sessions when they were being read to. The parents were told to give their children:

- more opportunities to talk;
- more encouragement for doing so; and
- better feedback.

For instance, parents were advised to encourage children to talk about the contents of the books that were being read to them, rather than just looking and listening. To encourage children to participate more actively in the reading sessions and express their thoughts in language, parents were told to ask various "What?" and "Why?" questions, such as "There's Eeyore. What's happening to him?" or "Why do you think the little girl is running after the bunny?". The parents were also given other kinds of advice about ways to encourage their children to express themselves in words, and ways to respond to their children's efforts. For instance, they were advised to introduce unfamiliar kinds of questions in a graduated way, thus making progressively greater demands on their child's active use of language.

The reading sessions were recorded on tape. This made it possible for the experimenters who were providing the parental training to assess the extent to which particular parents were successful in actually implementing the procedures that they were learning to introduce.

At the end of a month the children's language skills were tested. Another test was administered nine months later, to discover whether the programme had any long-term effects. The findings were very promising, despite the fact that the intervention was a relatively modest and economical one, involving a limited amount of daily time over a fairly brief period, and requiring only one hour of direct instruction for the participating parents. On two standard language tests, scores of the children who had received special training were, on average, six to eight months ahead of those of the children in the control group. These children were still ahead of the others when they were tested again nine months afterwards.

Photograph courtesy TRIP, photographer H. Rogers

The findings of the investigations conducted by the research teams headed by William Fowler and Grover Whitehurst suggest that it is indeed possible for parents to take steps that will accelerate their children's acquisition of language skills. Some other investigations have reached similar conclusions. However, as we have seen, it is also true that even those children who receive no special encouragement do eventually master their own language, to some degree at least. It could be therefore be argued that even if children can be helped to acquire language earlier than usual, it is not necessarily useful for them to do so. So we need to answer the question, even if language acceleration is possible, does it actually convey any real advantage? As it happens, there are a number of reasons why children do benefit, often very considerably, from being encouraged to make better than average progress at mastering language:

- The first reason is that, as was mentioned earlier, acquiring a language helps a child in a number of very useful ways. As well as making it possible for people to communicate with one another, language opens doors to many other essential activities. Language is needed in order for a person to do many of the things that daily living requires, such as reasoning, thinking and solving problems, and remembering the past and making plans for the future.

- Second, although having the barely adequate command of language that is likely to be acquired by a young person whose parents make no effort to encourage the child to gain language skills may be enough for some purposes, it is increasingly necessary for people today to have a good mastery of their own language. People need more than barely adequate language skills. In the past, when work was largely of a physical nature and many people's jobs were unskilled, for many individuals sophisticated language skills were not essential. But that is no longer true. People living in a complex world constantly depend on linguistic information, and someone whose capacity for understanding or self-expression is restricted will be at a real disadvantage.

- Third, children whose language skills are defective are particularly at risk when they are trying to learn to read, as we shall see in the following section. For a child to be able to learn to read, the kind of minimal language expertise that enables a child to "get by" in everyday life proves glaringly inadequate.

Reading

Like acquiring language, gaining the ability to read is important for a child because it opens doors to many opportunities. It helps children to learn further skills and add to their knowledge. A particularly important consequence of learning to read is that it makes a child more independent as a learner. Instead of always having to depend on adults to provide the information and guidance that make new learning possible, the child who can read can take a more active and independent role. She can now find new information for herself, and expand her knowledge and skills without always depending on other people, such as parents and teachers.

Also, in learning to read we become members of a culture of literacy. This is something that we are rarely aware of, because we remember very little of what our lives were like prior to the time when we became able to read. But reading does fundamentally change our lives. For instance, even a common and taken-for-granted concept such as a word may have little meaning for someone who cannot read. And a person who is unable to discern how the stream of language is made up of words and phrases will be prone to making errors in understanding what people are saying and in recalling new information.

Is it helpful to learn to read especially early? Reading certainly brings a child some useful advantages. However, the positive consequences of early reading are usually relatively small in comparison with the negative outcomes of being a severely backward reader. For that reason some experts advise the parents of young children not to be overly concerned to encourage early reading in their child. What is far more important is to give priority to helping the child to avoid serious problems when reading instruction does begin.

A large number of children do experience major difficulties in learning to read. Occasionally the causes of such difficulties are a mystery, or stem from abnormal functioning of the brain. In most cases, however, there is nothing at all mysterious involved. The most common reason why some children encounter problems in connection with learning to read is simply that reading is a difficult achievement.

Mastering reading is a big step for the young learner. This is partly because a number of different sub-skills have to be gained. In addition to that, the beginning reader has to retain in memory substantial amounts of information about letters and words. And these are not the only reasons why learning to read is difficult. Some of the other difficulties become clearer if we try to recall our own experiences in mastering a more recently acquired ability. Take driving, for example. Of course, learning to read and learning to drive are very different accomplishments. Nevertheless there are some illuminating parallels, and they do have elements in common. For instance, driving and reading both depend on the learner acquiring a number of component abilities, which have to be used in combination. In reading, like driving, there are numerous ways in which learners can go wrong. In both cases there are many possible reasons for a person to experience difficulties.

In some ways the young would-be reader's learning task is much harder than that of the learner driver. The beginner feels that a number of different things have to be attended to at more or less the same time, and unlike the experienced person, the learner cannot enjoy the benefits that follow when acquired skills become automatic, and no longer demand the individual's full attention. With driving, the vast majority of learners can count on the advantages that follow from being highly motivated to succeed. In young children who are learning to read even that cannot always be taken for granted. This is especially true in the case of youngsters whose parents are infrequent readers themselves and rarely read to their children. For these young people their daily lives may provide few if any demonstrations of the enjoyment to be gained from reading. And they may be largely unaware of the practical advantages of being able to read.

So we should not be too surprised to find that some children experience difficulties with learning to read. And more importantly, when that happens we would be wrong to leap to the conclusion that the child must be suffering from some abnormal condition or disability, just as we would not leap to that kind of conclusion whenever someone finds driving difficult. For the struggling young reader, just like the struggling learner driver, what is usually needed is plenty of well designed and patient teaching, lots of practice, and sympathetic assistance that is designed to improve the learner's confidence and ensure that he or she is motivated to succeed.

Avoiding reading difficulties

At school, the children who are the least likely to experience major problems with learning to read are those whose home experiences have equipped them with a variety of the basic skills on which language builds. Language skills are particularly important here. Those youngsters who have a good mastery of their own language will have already acquired a number of the basic capabilities that a would-be reader needs.

In contrast, children whose language development is restricted, and are not used to listening to words carefully, often find it hard to make good progress at reading. One reason for this is that in reading, unlike most of the situations a child encounters in daily life, it is essential for a child to be able to make fine discriminations between words that sound quite similar, such as *bed, red, said, dead, led* , or between *when, wet, where*. The lack of experience in making such discriminations is a major cause of serious reading problems in children (Bryant & Bradley, 1985).

When children who cannot tell similar words apart are trying to learn to read, they experience real difficulties. The reason for this is because reading is almost impossible unless a person hears language accurately enough to be able to distinguish between similar sounds such as the *b* in bad and the *d* in dad. A child who is regularly read to by his parents will have had numerous opportunities to learn to make such fine distinctions. That is particularly true if the child has been given plenty of opportunities to listen to rhymes and poems. These, by their very nature, direct attention to the precise sounds of words. However, a child who has had few experiences of being read to may not have been exposed to the kinds of learning experiences that equip a young person for distinguishing between similar word sounds.

Children whose home experiences of listening to language have been restricted may need special help, if they are to avoid having difficulties in learning to read. In the study conducted by Peter Bryant and Lynette Bradley, children aged 4 listened to lists containing three words, two of which had a sound in common. They had to say which word was the odd one out. A typical list was *dig dot bun*. Four years later, the same children were tested at reading. At this later time it was discovered that most of the 4-year-olds who had done well at the task had become adequate readers for their age, but those who had done poorly at it were likely to be poor readers.

In the next stage of their investigation, Bryant and Bradley gave special remedial training in discriminating between sounds to 4- and 5-year-olds who did poorly at the word task. When these children were tested four years later they were found to be making normal progress at reading. However, those children who did poorly at the test but subsequently had not received special help lagged a year behind.

The kind of remedial training introduced by Bryant and Bradley is not needed by children whose parents regularly read to them. This is because through listening to a parent read aloud a child gains various listening skills and other language capabilities that prepare a young person for mastering reading. What else can parents do to help ensure that their child is adequately prepared for learning to read, apart from reading aloud to the child? There are three broad ways in which parents can help:

- They can make sure that their child grows up in an environment that is rich in written or printed information, and in which the child is given opportunities to observe that reading makes a contribution to people's daily lives. Parents can help to make the child aware of the value of reading by drawing attention to the various uses of reading and writing, for example by explaining the words on a tube of toothpaste or a medicine bottle, or demonstrating how the daily newspaper provides information about what programmes are on television.
- Parents can demonstrate to their children that reading is something that gives enjoyment to people, for example by showing how they are enjoying a book, or by sharing a joke or news item from a magazine.

- It is useful to encourage a child to gain pre-reading skills such as the capacity to write letters of the alphabet. Games and play activities can provide ways to teach young children about letters.

Approaches to reading instruction

Over the years there have been various controversies about the relative effectiveness of different methods for teaching reading. In fact, the search for a "best" method may be fruitless: the chances are that there is no one technique that is most successful for all children.

- One teaching approach, called *phonics*, involves placing emphasis on learning to decode words. The child works out how a word sounds by applying knowledge of the separate sounds of the elements making up the word.
- In the other common approach, known as *look and say* (or "whole word" or "sight"), the child does not decode but learns to identify whole words on the basis of their appearance.

Rather than regarding phonics and look and say as alternative teaching methods, it is more sensible to regard them as being different but complementary approaches. Each has a role in learning to read. Each has advantages and limitations.

The approach underlying phonics is in some respects particularly central to the task of mastering reading. The child who is instructed in phonics learns the rules that make it possible to identify how a word sounds. As a result, she becomes able to decode written language. A child who learns by look and say, on the other hand, only learns to identify particular words. He may fail to acquire skills that are needed to work out the sound of unfamiliar words, or ones whose sounds or meanings have been forgotten.

Considered in that way, the phonics approach seems to be clearly superior to look and say, because only the former enables the child to acquire general reading skills rather than just being able to identify particular words. Up to a point that is true. However, the phonics approach has limitations of its own. A particular problem is that, for the beginning reader, learning that depends on phonics alone is likely to be extremely slow at first, and this can be very dispiriting. However, if the young reader has already gained a small vocabulary of common words which she has learned to identify through the use of the look and say approach, initial progress will be faster. As a result, it will be much easier to get to the point at which simple books can be read and enjoyed. So a certain amount of look and say word learning at an early stage of the process of learning to read will help get the young would-be reader off the ground. This will help to motivate the would-be reader by making it possible to have the experience of actually reading simple materials fairly fluently, well before that would have been possible with a teaching method that was confined to phonics alone.

As well as the decoding that is made possible by phonics learning and the word identification that is achieved by a look and say approach, young readers help themselves to read in other ways. For example, a child who is trying to read an unfamiliar word may notice a similarity with a word that is already familiar. A child who encounters the word *tight* for the first time, but already knows *light* and *sight*, may be able to work out the sound of the new item, through reasoning that *ight* is likely to sound the same in the new word as it does in the familiar ones. By making *analogies* of this kind children are able to augment their decoding skills and extend their reading vocabularies.

The beginnings of numeracy

To gain number skills and make progress at arithmetic, a child needs to be able to count and has to know about the relationships between different quantities. For example, relations such as "same", "larger" and "smaller" have to be understood. But even babies have some understanding of number relations. For example, children aged 8 months notice when they are shown an outcome of adding to or subtracting from a group of toys that is different from the actual result that would be predicted on the basis of simple addition or subtraction. In a study by Karen Wynn children were shown a Mickey Mouse toy, and they next saw the toy being placed behind a screen (Wynn, 1992). Then the children saw another Mickey Mouse toy being placed behind the screen. On other occasions children were shown two toys, which they then saw being placed behind a screen, and later observed one of the toys being removed. In each instance the screen was finally taken away. On some occasions, but not others, the number of toys that was now displayed was the correct outcome of the adding or subtracting operations that the children had watched. For example, when the children had been shown one toy, and then another doll had been added, removal of the screen might reveal two toys. In other instances the number of dolls that were revealed when the screen was removed was more or less than it should have been. At this stage of the experiment it was found that children responded differently according to whether or not the appropriate number of toys was revealed when the screen was removed. This suggests that even at the age of 8 months babies can tell whether or not simple additions have been correctly performed.

Children begin to count at around the age of 2. Adults can be misled by the sight of a confident 2- or 3-year-old reciting "one, two, three…" into believing that the child has a full understanding of how to count. It is true that even very young children seem to have some basic understanding of quantities, and by the age of about 3 they are capable of at least some of the operations involved in counting. All the same, it takes a fair amount of time and experience to gain a reasonable understanding of numbers. There is a very large difference between simply being able to recite number labels and being able to understand what numbers really are.

Children thrive on opportunities to practise their counting skills, but too much pressure to count conventionally may cause frustration. Also, having to count considerably larger sets of items than a child is used to may be too difficult, because this can overload the child's

memory. Adults should avoid discouraging children from using the strategies they are comfortable with, even ones that seem crude and unsophisticated, such as counting aloud, pointing, using fingers, and touching objects. All these activities help the child to deal with tasks that are difficult and demand close attention and concentration. Eventually, as counting becomes more routinised and automatic, it demands less of the child's attention, and these aids are gradually discarded as the child finds them less necessary. But there is no point in trying to hurry this process.

As Rachel Gelman has explained, in order to count properly and understand what is being done, a child needs to grasp five basic principles. The first involves seeing the necessity to count each object in the set once and only once. The second is that counting proceeds in a fixed order, "one , two, three...", rather than being simply a random sequence of numbers. The third principle involves knowing that the final number counted represents the value of the set. The fourth principle is that the number of items in the set is independent of the attributes or quality of the item. So, for example, the fact that one object is particularly large or is an unusual colour has to be ignored when the objects are being counted. The fifth and final principle is that the actual order in which the items in a set are being counted makes no difference: irrespective of which object one starts with, the total number remains the same.

Proper counting depends on the individual having some appreciation of the fact that numbers do not just relate to particular things and objects, but to quantities in general. For a young child, this idea is quite an abstract one, and it is only mastered after the child has had plenty of practical experience with the various kinds of activities that are involved in counting. In one series of investigations, 3-year-olds were required to sort cards on the basis of the number of items depicted on them (Gelman, 1978). The cards also contained various potentially distracting kinds of information, such as the length and density of the items. Gelman found that most of the children were capable of grouping the cards by number, so long as the number did not exceed two or three. When the number of elements was higher, however, the children were likely to be distracted by other information on the cards, such as the length of the visual array of objects. But even at the age of 3, children did notice when the number of objects in a visual display was changed, even

Photograph courtesy of TRIP, photographer H. Rogers

if the other aspects of the display that usually accompany such a change, such as size and density, were left unaltered.

Having numerous and varied experiences with different quantities of real objects allows children to become increasingly familiar with numbers. Children need to learn by discovering things for themselves. The young child who has calculated that two eggs plus another three eggs makes five eggs may not realise that two apples plus three apples makes five apples until she has discovered that for herself. As with numbers, learning to understand the general rules of arithmetic and how they work takes time, and requires plenty of practical experience. This needs to involve actual physical objects, at least in the early stages.

There are plenty of games and activities that parents of pre-school children can introduce in order to encourage a child to practise number skills. Counting can often play a part in other play activities, and in reading to a baby there will usually be opportunities to count objects. Fetching or "shopping" play activities can easily be made to emphasise counting, and it is worth noting that language activities and counting games can often be combined: the two are by no means mutually exclusive. The more numerous and varied the situations in which a child encounters numbers and counting, the better.

Addition and subtracting build on counting. It is possible to count just by combining counting operations. For instance, to add 3+4 it is possible to simply count up to 3 and then go on counting by another four items. With actual objects that method of counting all the items works well enough, even if it is a slow and uneconomical way of adding. A more effective method of simple addition is to start with one of the numbers, and then count on. Counting on in this way means that only one of the sets of numbers has to be counted. A slightly more sophisticated variant involves realising that it is more sensible to count on from the higher number rather than just taking either of the original numbers at random and counting on from there. Clearly, for example, if the numbers to be added were 6+2, counting on from 6 would be considerably less time-consuming than counting on from 2.

Most children reach the stage of counting on from the large number during their first two years at school, and appropriate teaching can accelerate their progress. When addition and subtraction have been mastered, multiplication can be introduced. However, children find multiplication and division considerably more difficult than addition and subtraction. Although it is possible to solve multiplication problems by repeated addition, it is easy to go astray. Again, opportunities to practice should be plentiful, with an absence of pressure to move ahead too quickly.

Physical skills

Just as the capability to acquire language seems to be innately specified in humans, gaining the capacity to walk, sit, and move our bodies also appears to happen naturally. Babies learn to walk without having to engage in the lengthy and deliberate learning activities that are necessary for some other accomplishments, such as reading. However, as in the case of language learning, that does not mean that variations in the richness and variety of learning experiences make no difference.

For example, Charles Super (1976) discovered that Kenyan children from the same tribe differ enormously in the age at which they begin walking, sitting without support, and standing, in ways that are closely related to their early experiences. Children brought up in traditional villages where these skills are deliberately taught, acquire these motor capabilities a month or so earlier than most children in other continents. However, children from the same tribe who are brought up in an urban environment—where parents do not provide the special training given in traditional villages—are not at all advanced in those motor skills at which the traditionally raised infants excel. The primary cause of the traditionally raised infants' precocity appears to lie in the special training they are given. This is demonstrated by the finding that there was a strong relationship between the age at which babies began to crawl and a measure of the extent to which the parents provided opportunities designed to encourage crawling. In other words, early crawling was associated with high levels of encouragement.

These results demonstrate that special efforts to encourage babies to gain physical skills can make a real difference, even as early as the first year. It is not clear from Super's study whether or not the effects are long lasting, but evidence from other studies suggests that early training at physical skills may have effects that endure for years, and perhaps permanently. For instance, in a study conducted in the 1920s one of a pair of twin girls was taught a number of physical skills, including climbing stairs, when she was 10 months old. Her twin sister was given the same training, but not until seven weeks later. It was initially reported that by the second week of her training the second twin had practically caught up (Gesell & Thompson, 1929). Yet a closer examination of the findings revealed clear evidence that the early training did have a long-lasting and substantial influence (Fowler, 1983). For instance, the first-taught child's level of performance at a task requiring the delicate control of toy blocks was never equalled by the other twin. Also, the child who was trained first performed better at the majority of the other physical skills that the twins were taught. She was still superior when follow-up tests were given one month after the second twin had been trained, and again two months after that. Even many years later, when the twins were teenagers, the sister who was the first to be trained was still better than her twin at a number of movement-based abilities, such as tap-dancing, running, and walking.

The continuing difference between the twins was all the more remarkable considering that the length of special training they had been given was distinctly short. For example, the sessions of stair-climbing instruction involved only 20 minutes per day, over a six-week period of time. It also emerged that *both* of the twins made better than average progress at the skills in which they had been instructed. Even the twin who was trained at stair-climbing for just two weeks could climb five stairs on her own in ten seconds at the age of 1 year, a feat that the average child could not match until the age of 2.

As these findings were based on a single pair of twins we cannot draw any really firm conclusions from them. However, additional research findings provide further evidence that early training in physical skills can have substantial and long-lasting outcomes. In one investigation different amounts of early training were given to two male twins. One had instruction in a number of physical skills between the ages of 7 months and 24 months, on five days each week. The other received less than three months' training, starting considerably later, when he was 22 months old (McGraw 1935, 1939). As in the other study, the different regimes of early childhood encouragement led to large and permanent differences between the twins in their physical expertise. The twin who received earlier and more intensive training made excellent progress. His performance was well above the average for boys of his age, and also much better than that of his twin brother. For instance, the first twin swam at 10 months and could dive from a diving-board at 17 months. At 6 years of age he was still well ahead of his brother. Even when they reached the age of 22 the first twin still displayed greater ability, and was more confident and enthusiastic than his brother at physical skills such as climbing a ladder.

Studies conducted more recently confirm these findings. They show that carefully planned early training programmes can lead to substantial gains. In one study nursery school children who were given training over an eight-week period in skills such as kicking, long jumping, bouncing a ball, and balancing on a board, achieved real gains compared with children in a comparison group who received no special training. William Fowler and his colleagues found that 4-year-olds who were given three 30-minute training sessions in gymnastic skills each week, over a 15-week period, made big advances (Fowler et al.,

1983). Their gains were five times as large as the ones made by children who received no gymnastics training during the same period of time. However, the advances were fairly specific: the trained children were no better than the others at physical tasks other than the gymnastic skills that they had practised. Clearly, it cannot be assumed that a new skill will automatically "transfer" to different tasks.

Advantages and disadvantages of accelerated early learning

Most questions about accelerating early learning fall into one of two broad categories. These are:

- First, queries about the *possibility* of accelerating progress in a young child.
- Second, queries about the *desirability* of doing so.

So far as questions within the first category are concerned, the answers are mostly positive, as we have already seen. Research findings demonstrate that it is definitely possible to take steps that will improve the quality of language skills in young children. That is despite the fact that we humans are designed in a way that helps to make first-language learning relatively easy and natural for the majority of children. A child's progress in other areas of competence, including reading, ability with numbers, and physical skills, can also be accelerated, if

parents or other adults are able to provide special encouragement and support and plenty of opportunities to learn.

Incidentally, it has also been found that *depriving* babies and young children of stimulation actively *retards* early learning. Apart from the many survey investigations that have demonstrated this, there have been occasional experimental studies of the effects of deprivation. One investigation was undertaken by a husband and wife team in the 1930s (Dennis & Dennis, 1951). These researchers looked after a pair of non-identical twins from the end of their first month to the fourteenth month. The twins received no stimulation beyond what was necessary for physical care. They were fed, changed, kept warm, but given no toys. How did this regime affect the twins? The researchers discovered that up to the age of 7 months their scores at developmental tests were more or less normal, but later development was seriously retarded.

By showing that early deprivation can retard development, just as early training and encouragement can accelerate it, the Dennis and Dennis study provides further evidence of powerful effects of experience in the early years. The results were obtained despite the fact that the twins actually received two hours of undivided attention each day during the period of deprivation, which is more than many babies experience. Subsequently, both twins were given extra training, and their developmental progress then returned to normal.

But even if acceleration is possible, is it necessarily desirable? As we have seen, there are certainly some positive consequences of acquiring basic skills earlier than usual. For instance, a young child who has above-average language mastery will be unlikely to experience difficulties in learning to read. Similarly, a child who reads earlier than usual will benefit from being unusually well equipped to learn independently. Yet efforts to accelerate early learning can also have negative outcomes. For example, the over-enthusiasm of parents who are concerned to make their child brighter or cleverer than other youngsters can lead to the child feeling pushed or pressurised to do well, and anxious about the possibility of failing to meet parental expectations.

Not all parents succeed in drawing the line between encouraging young children and pushing them. Too much pressure can certainly be harmful and discouraging, and children tend to react badly if they feel that they are being criticised or constantly tested. Adults sometimes fail to appreciate that young children have short attention spans. On occasions they become tired of a particular activity or bored with it.

Parents need to be aware that when that happens it is useless to persist with efforts to teach them.

Generally speaking, provided that parents' efforts to encourage young children to learn always talk the form of activities that are playful, informal, and in tune with children's preferences, the problems associated with too much pressure are likely to be avoided. Yet some difficulties can arise even when adults are careful to ensure that children are only encouraged to engage in learning activities when they are genuinely keen to do so. One source of possible difficulties is the fact that parents who are anxious to help a child to succeed may place so much emphasis on learning games and activities that they inadvertently deprive the child of other necessary childhood experiences.

There are various activities and experiences that may not appear to be rich in educational value but which may still make a big contribution to the child's development. For example, young children need to have opportunities to play with other children. It is particularly important for them to be able to share experiences with others. Activities of this kind provide the situations in which young people acquire important social skills and learn how to make friendships and gain a shared sense of humour. But for some youngsters, their parents' strong commitment to early childhood learning may result in the child being submitted to a "hothouse" kind of daily regime, which restricts opportunities to engage in everyday activities involving play with other children. These young people may end up being deprived of ordinary daily experiences that contribute to healthy emotional and social development.

How can parents of young children make sure that a child receives the benefits of being encouraged to learn while avoiding the possible ill-effects? Following these broad guidelines, taken from *Give your child a better start*, by Michael Howe and Harriet Griffey, published by Penguin Books (1995) will help to make this possible.

- Do things together.
- Make sure that there are times when your child has all your attention.
- Share your everyday activities with your children: include them in as much as possible of your daily life.
- Talk *with* your children, not *at* them, and have plenty of dialogues in which you and the child can respond to one another.

- Enjoy lots of games together.
- Never criticize your young child's efforts.
- Make a big effort to see life from your child's point of view.
- Be serious about guiding your child towards learning and discovery.

Compensating for early deprivation

Some parents fail to give their children the support and encouragement that leads to the acquisition of a firm foundation for basic abilities that they can draw on as they get older and which enable them to thrive in the school classroom. A few parents simply do not care enough. Others, perhaps because the parenting they received themselves was less than ideal, fail to appreciate that every child requires plenty of attention, support, and encouragement in order to thrive. Other parents, because of poverty, ignorance, poor mental health, or lack of time and energy, are just not able to give enough attention to their children's learning needs.

There are serious possible consequences of a child failing to gain fundamental capabilities in the early years. These include reading difficulties and other kinds of school failure in the short run, and a lack of qualifications and job skills in the longer run. In an attempt to ameliorate these problems, various programmes have been devised which aim to provide "compensatory" experiences for educationally deprived young children. The children who participate in these programmes are given learning experiences that they would otherwise lack.

In particular, from 1965 onwards, many pre-school children from poor homes in the United States attended "Head Start" classes. These were designed to provide compensatory early education, emphasising language skills in particular. In addition, the programmes helped to equip children with numeracy and other basic abilities that help a child become prepared to take advantage of those learning opportunities that are provided when the child goes to school.

Head Start programmes have varied considerably in quality and intensity. Some have been well funded and taught by experts, with small numbers of children to each teacher. Other programmes have involved inadequately trained teachers working with too many children in poor conditions. Some programmes have involved no more than two mornings or afternoons per week during a single summer, whereas others have been considerably longer or more intensive. In some compensatory programmes only the child has been helped. In others, including some of the most successful, there have been frequent home visits, and parents have been given support and training aimed at helping them to play a more positive role in encouraging their child to gain language skills and other capabilities (Wasik, Ramey, Bryant, & Sparling, 1990).

Not surprisingly, in view of their diversity, there has been considerable variability in the extent to which Head Start programmes have succeeded in their aim of compensating for the ill-effects of early deprivation. Generally speaking, the better and more intensive programmes have been highly successful, according to various indicators, such as children succeeding at school to a greater extent than comparable children who did not attend Head Start classes, or by higher employment levels later in life, or by higher IQ (Intelligence Quotient) scores in intelligence tests.

Criticisms of Head Start

Critics have pointed out that some of the gains from Head Start programmes have been temporary, tending to decrease or "fade" after several years. They have also drawn attention to the fact that not all Head Start programmes have led to substantial gains. However, advocates of compensatory early education have found both those criticisms easy to refute.

In response to the observation that gains sometimes fade, it has been pointed out that under certain circumstances newly gained skills and abilities almost always do fade. In particular, if a person does not have opportunities to practise using a new skill, and gain a habit of using it, and have the experience of finding the skill a useful or beneficial one, the chances are that it will indeed fade. Unfortunately, circumstances like that are all too commonly encountered by children who have attended Head Start classes. For many children whose basic abilities have been extended and whose IQ scores have increased following involvement in an intervention programme, the combined effects of living in ghetto communities often characterised by urban squalor, bad housing, drug abuse, violence, and massive unemployment, with poor schooling and restricted family life, have resulted in very few opportunities for the children to use or extend their newly gained capabilities (Howe, 1997).

The problems have been compounded by the fact that the schools subsequently attended by children who have been in Head Start programmes have often been ones that were unsafe and did not provide a stimulating educational climate, with low average achievements and very limited resources. In circumstances like this it is almost inevitable that a child's new knowledge and skills will fade. So the fact that fading of newly gained skills and knowledge does sometimes occur does not mean that there was something defective in the intervention programme. Nor does it mean that fading is inevitable. It does, however, mean that the compensatory learning experiences provided in a short programme may need to be supplemented with continuing opportunities and encouragement, if their positive effects are not to become diluted.

Compensatory education. Why do the improvements sometimes fade?

An investigation conducted by Victoria Seitz was designed to discover why some of the improvements produced by Head Start programmes tended to diminish over a period of years. She assessed the outcomes of a four-year educational intervention programme that emphasised mathematical skills. Inner-city boys participated, beginning in kindergarten (Zigler & Seitz, 1982). The programme had been highly effective at first, but in a follow-up study, continued over several years, the large improvement in the boys who had taken part gradually diminished, compared with a control group. At the end of the programme the participants were two years ahead, but by the age of 15 or so they were only one year ahead.

Seitz took steps to find out why this fading was taking place. She found no evidence of a loss of basic mathematical ability. Yet she discovered that the older boys were simply not being taught the kinds of mathematical skills that they would need in order to keep making good progress. For instance, to score well at the achievement tests used with older children it is essential to know about algebra and geometry. Seitz found, however, that unlike the majority of children who attend schools in middle-class areas, the disadvantaged pupils were simply not getting the necessary teaching. So they could hardly have been expected to do well. The true picture was not one of fading basic ability but of diminishing practice opportunities to learn.

The second common criticism of compensatory programmes such as the Head Start ones is that not all programmes have been highly successful. That is true enough, although in view of their limitations and defects it would be somewhat amazing if they were all effective. Many of these programmes have been of very short duration, with extremely restricted budgets and inadequate numbers of staff, and the staff have not always been adequately trained.

The kinds of learning experiences that do make a real difference in someone's life almost always require a substantial investment of time. In music, for example, it takes a young performing instrumentalist about 3500 hours practising, on average, to reach the standard of a good amateur musician (Grade Eight of the musical board examinations). Comparable amounts of training are needed in order to reach high levels of expertise in other skill areas such as chess and various sports, or in foreign languages. Reaching professional standards takes even longer. Consequently, in order for a Head Start programme to have a good chance of being successful at giving a child compensatory educational experiences, it would need to be intensive and continue over a lengthy period of time. Yet most of the programmes that have been evaluated have been of short duration and not intensive at all. Very few have involved anything like the amount of instruction and practice that is recognised to be essential with skills such as music. A typical one-summer Head Start programme, for instance, would last for ten weeks, with three two-hour sessions per week. Here the total investment for each child would have been no more than 60 hours, a very brief period of time in relation to the one just quoted.

Miracles apart, a programme lasting no more than 60 hours could hardly be expected to make more than a puny impact on a child. Compare that 60-hour period with the actual real-life variations in everyday experiences that accompany differences between young children in their capabilities. For instance, in one large-scale study of child language it was discovered that in just one typical week the number of words 3-year-old children from varying social classes experienced differed by as much as 150,000. By the age of 3, children in professional families had heard more than 30 million words. In contrast, children from the poorest families had heard only around 10 million words directed at them (Hart & Risley, 1995). These data make it clear that underlying the differences between children in their language skills were huge and long-lasting differences in their language experiences. In other words, these "naturally occurring" differences in children's early learning experiences are vast in relation to the small magnitude of the kinds of interventions that have been introduced with compensatory education programmes.

Taking into account the restricted durations of Head Start programmes, as well as the fact that the majority of them have involved group rather than individual instruction, often by teachers who were not highly qualified or experienced, some of the gains have actually been remarkably impressive. In a substantial number of intervention studies there have been large IQ gains and various other kinds of improved progress. That is in spite the fact that the duration and magnitude of the compensatory experiences were so small in relation to the variations in children's everyday life experiences just described. So there is rather conclusive evidence that compensatory efforts can be highly effective.

Getting prepared for school

In a child's earliest years, the circumstances in which children typically extend their capabilities are informal ones, based on the home and the family. That changes when a child starts attending school. From then onwards, gaining new knowledge and skills is more likely to depend on deliberate and more formal learning activities, often directed by a teacher.

Two children who start school at the same time may be equally bright, knowledgeable, and quick-witted, and yet unequally prepared

---

Learning at home and learning at school. Some key differences

Imagine a child who is going to school for the first time. He discovers that school makes demands on him that are different from anything he has experienced at home. For example:

- There are no familiar parents or other family members to depend on for help when it is needed. The only adults to be seen are relative strangers, and they are struggling to meet the needs of a large number of children.
- There are frequent activities in which a child is expected to learn this or remember that just for its own sake, without there being any obvious reason. Some children may only have a hazy idea of what the teacher actually means when she tells them she wants them to remember something.

- The classroom may be a noisy environment, but nevertheless a child is expected to concentrate on what the teacher is saying. Unlike parents, the teacher is unlikely to notice if a particular child fails to hear or understand what is said.
- At school, unlike at home, it is not usually possible for a child to stop what he is doing and move on to a different activity when he gets tired or bored. Having to sit still and concentrate is a requirement many children's home lives may not have prepared them for.

---

to thrive in the new and unfamiliar kind of learning environment that a youngster encounters at school. Why is that? A common reason is that while the two children's family backgrounds may have been equally stimulating and loving, and perhaps equally conducive to the kinds of learning that made it possible to gain capacities needed in everyday living, they may have been very unequal in the extent to which they

Photograph
courtesy TRIP,
photographer
H. Rogers

have succeeded in preparing the child for learning in the different circumstances of the school classroom.

There are two broad ways in which home learning experiences help a child to be ready to make the most of school.

- First, as we have seen earlier in this chapter, there are skills and knowledge that may be gained at home and can be drawn upon at school. These include knowledge of letters and simple number skills.
- Second, a child may begin at home to " learn how to learn" by gaining useful habits that aid learning (such as listening carefully) and simple learning strategies, such as rehearsing. As was mentioned in the previous chapter, a child who has acquired the habit of rehearsing will do better at school than a child who has not.

For some children, life at home with their parents will have included experiences that do much to make a child ready to meet these new demands of life at school. These will tend to be children whose parents are well educated and informed about the deliberate kinds of learning activities that help a child to succeed at school. For other children, however, home life may have included rather few of the experiences that make a child prepared for school.

Summary

Learning begins to affect babies' capacities in the first months of life. At this time it can take forms similar to those found in non-human species, including classical conditioning, operant conditioning, habituation, and imitative learning.

Language expands our capacities enormously: it plays a large part in setting humans apart from other species. Our ability to acquire language depends on the fact that human brains are designed to make rapid language learning possible. Nevertheless, various pre-language abilities have to be gained, through learning, to prepare the young child for acquiring language. Children thrive in language-rich environments. They benefit from being encouraged by their parents to make better than average progress at acquiring language.

Reading, like language, opens doors to the acquisition of other important capacities. It helps to make a learner more independent. Numeracy is also important, and depends on a child having numerous concrete experiences involving quantities. The early acquisition of physical skills is strongly influenced by the nature of a child's experiences.

Accelerated early learning can bring clear benefits, although insensitive efforts to teach young children can be sometimes be harmful. Efforts to provide compensatory education for children whose early home environments have failed to provide support and encouragement for learning have proved highly successful when they are well designed and adequately funded. The kinds of early learning opportunities a child is exposed to are important in preparing the child for learning at school.

Further reading

The child's acquisition of cognitive abilities is described in S. Meadows (1993), *The child as a thinker*, (London: Routledge), and S. Meadows (1996), *Parenting behaviour and children's cognitive development* (Hove, UK: Psychology Press). A convincing account of the importance of the home background in encouraging language development is provided by B. Hart and T. Risley (1995), *Meaningful differences in everyday parenting and intellectual development in young American children* (Baltimore: Brookes). For a practical account of the ways in which parents can encourage young children to learn, see M.J.A. Howe & H. Griffey, (1995), *Give your child a better start: How to encourage early learning* (London: Penguin).

People's abilities: What are they? 3

Up to now, although various kinds of skills, knowledge, and capabilities have been discussed, little has been said about abilities in general. No effort has been made to specify what is meant by that word, or to enquire into the actual nature of abilities and the form they take. We remedy this in the present chapter. It takes a broad look at human abilities and raises a number of questions about them. We ask, for instance:

- What are abilities?
- How fixed are they?
- To what extent do different abilities influence one another?
- Do a person's specific capacities depend on an underlying general ability?

What is an ability?

There is no single right answer to the question "What is an ability?" It can be a skill, or a capacity to think, or a capability that is largely based on someone's knowledge, or a combination of any of these. An ability can be broad, as indicated when psychologists introduce terms such as "verbal ability" or "motor ability", or it can be specific, as is implied when a person is said to have the ability to sail a boat or drive a car. People use the word in a variety of different ways. Even within psychology, there is variability in the meanings that different writers have in mind when they introduce the word "ability".

It is sometimes believed that every psychological concept must have a single correct definition, which we could discover if only we were clever enough to find it. But more often than not, this is untrue. Sometimes, the real meaning of a word or concept can vary, and depends on whatever it is that someone intends to communicate at a particular time. This is not to say that a single word can mean anything at all, or have a range of totally different meanings. The different possible meanings of the term are all fairly similar, even though there is no one precise meaning that is unequivocally more correct than any of the others.

One reason why the question "What is an ability?" is not an easy one to answer is that abilities are not object-like things that you can see or touch. In common with other psychological concepts, abilities are not physical items that can be directly observed or measured. Ability is an abstract concept. It refers to capacities that we deduce are present in a person. Typically, we do so after noticing that the person performs certain activities or behaviours.

For example, if someone is asked to add 2 + 2 and they give the correct answer, "4", we can say that the person has the ability to add those numbers. Strictly speaking, that is just an alternative way of saying that the person is capable of adding them. If the same person also provides the correct answer to a number of different addition problems, we might also deduce that he or she has a broad capacity (or ability) to add. And if the person succeeds at each of a range of adding, subtracting, multiplying and dividing problems, we regard that person as having ability to do arithmetic in general.

Note, however, that in these illustrations our saying that a person has an ability to do something is not very different from just noting that they are capable of doing it. We are not discovering anything about the person that we do not already know. All we have done is to introduce an abstract word.

It is especially important to appreciate that saying that a person has the ability to perform an action does not explain *why* they can do it. So although we may appear to be providing an explanation when we say that (for instance) the reason why Frank does better than Frances at a maths problem is because he has more mathematical ability, in reality all that is actually being said is that he has what it takes to solve the problem. Similarly, all that is achieved by listing someone's various abilities is to specify what that person can do — it offers nothing in the way of explanation.

How many different abilities?

Another question about abilities , "How many are there?", has no uniquely correct answer. Here the problem is that there are many possible answers, and no way to decide that one of them is more correct than the others.

One legitimate way of thinking of an ability is as a very broad capacity that encompasses a whole collection of distinct capabilities. That use of the term "ability" is often encountered in *psychometrics*, the branch of science concerned with the measurement of psychological characteristics. Here a division is sometimes made between just two kinds of ability, "verbal ability" and "non-verbal ability". The first of those terms refers to a person's general capacity to solve intellectual problems and do tasks that involve the use of language, and the second refers to a person's capacity to perform non-language tasks.

However, it is just as legitimate to use the word "ability" to denote capabilities that are considerably narrower and more specific. For example, it would be possible to make a short list of fairly general abilities, and include items such as numerical ability, spatial ability, social ability, musical ability, sporting ability, and so on. Or we might choose to make a longer list of even more specific abilities, such as walking, sitting, climbing, teeth-brushing, crossword-solving, car-driving and so on.

Some people believe that verbal and non-verbal ability can be regarded as *underlying* capacities that are necessary in order for more specific capabilities to be gained. However, there are no strong logical or empirical grounds for assuming that general abilities are necessarily more fundamental than more specific abilities.

You may find it surprising that "ability" is such a fuzzy concept, rather than having a single precise meaning. This may seem frustrating, but there is no need to feel alarmed about it. Yet it is important to keep remembering that saying that a person has the ability to do something does not explain *why* they can do it.

Are abilities fixed or fluid?

At first sight this question may seem rather silly. Of course abilities must be fixed: a person is either able or unable to answer a particular question or solve a problem. In fact, however, things are not that simple. By way of illustration, here is a true story about a mentally handicapped man. The man had been trained to operate a complex piece of industrial machinery, and eventually became capable of doing the job very efficiently. But one day a cleaner accidentally altered the position of the man's machine. It was turned by only a few degrees, and yet the change had the effect of making the man totally incapable of operating it. Could the man operate the machine or could he not? It is not possible to answer that question except by saying something like "It depends on ...".

Of course, that individual was unusual in having the limitations of being a mentally handicapped person. But as we shall see in the following pages, even in people of normal intelligence, the assumption that a person is either always capable or always incapable of doing something often turns out to be misguided. In particular, there are four kinds of influences that can make large differences to a person's capacity to perform tasks. These are:

1 Time and place.
2. The learner's mental state.
3. The personal significance of the task.
4. The way in which the problem is displayed.

The influence of time and place

The findings of some memory experiments provide evidence that abilities can be surprisingly fluid. In one investigation people were asked to examine a list of words, and their capacity to recall the words correctly was tested 24 hours later. The testing took place either in the same room as the one where they first encountered the words or in an entirely different room (Smith, 1979). This made a large difference. It was discovered that those participants who were tested in the original room recalled 50% more of the items than the other participants. Also, when people were tested in the different room, the accuracy of their recall improved if they were first instructed to think about the room in which the original learning had taken place.

These findings show that people's performance levels can be strongly affected by the particular situation, or "context", in which testing takes place. Recall was most accurate when the circumstances of the testing situation closely matched the physical conditions in which the initial studying took place.

In another study, children were given a task that required them to keep an eye on a clock which was monitoring timed events (Ceci & Bronfenbrenner, 1985). Some of the children were told to remove cupcakes from an oven after 30 minutes had elapsed; others had to disconnect a battery charger from a motorcycle battery after a 30-minute period. During the waiting time the children were allowed to do other things, such as play video games. The investigators wanted to know how efficiently each child would cope with the tasks. It was found that there were big variations. Some children kept looking at the clock throughout the 30-minute period, leaving themselves with hardly any time for other activities. Other children were much more efficient: after the first few minutes these youngsters only looked at the clock every so often, until the last five minutes or so, when they began to inspect it more frequently. With their better monitoring strategy

these children had much more time than the others to spend on other activities.

The older children were slightly more likely than the younger ones to have a good clock-watching strategy, leaving them free to do other things. However, a much bigger influence than age was the situation in which the watching (or "monitoring") task had to be done. Some of the participating children performed the task in their own homes. For the other children, although the monitoring tasks were the same, they had to be done in the unfamiliar context of a research laboratory. The researchers discovered that those children who did the monitoring tasks in their own homes performed far more efficiently than the others, giving themselves more time to get on with other things they wanted to do.

The effects of a learner's mental state

The findings of investigations have pinpointed further ways in which matches and mismatches between the particular contexts in which information is learned and recalled can affect people's performance. For instance, in one study people saw a staged robbery, and afterwards had to try to identify the "criminal" who carried out the robbery (Malpass & Devine, 1981). Participants who witnessed the robbery were much more likely to identify the criminal correctly if they were encouraged to think about what they had been doing at the time, and to recall the room in which the event took place.

In other studies it was found that people's recall of information that was first perceived when the person was under the influence of a consciousness-changing drug such as alcohol or marijuana was most accurate if their state of mind when recall was tested matched their state of mind when the information was first presented. Participants did best if they were under the influence of a particular drug either on both of those occasions or on neither of them (see Eich, 1981). A number of experiments have shown that learners' mental states have similar effects on performance even when no drugs are present. For example, people who take part in learning experiments recall more if their mood at the time of retrieval matches their mood at the time they were first given the information to be remembered, whether that mood is a happy one or a depressed one (Davies, 1988).

The personal significance of tasks

These demonstrations that situation and context can affect a person's degree of success at a demanding task show that a person's abilities are far from being fixed and constant. It is not just in memory tasks that the observed degree of competence depends on the particular circumstances in which a person is being assessed. The contexts in which knowledge or skills are utilised can also affect people's capacity to solve problems drawing on other abilities. And as well as the physical location and the individual's mood or state, other aspects of the situation or context in which an ability has to be exercised can increase or reduce a person's capability.

One important influence is the manner in which a person's skills are assessed, taking into account that individual's interests or preferences. In one investigation, Julia Smith and myself (Howe & Smith, 1988; Howe, 1989) gave subtraction tasks to a 14-year-old boy who despite being mentally handicapped could solve difficult problems involving calendar dates. If he was asked to specify the day of the week on which a future or past date fell, he could provide the correct answer, usually within a few seconds.

We gave him a number of simple subtraction questions, such as "What is 26 minus 4?". He seemed to find these problems difficult: it took him a long time to reply and he often got the answer wrong. We thought that it might help if we made the questions more interesting for him by basing them on real physical items. So we asked, for example "If you had 26 apples and someone took 4 away, how many would be left?". This change helped a little, but not much: the boy's performance was still poor. Finally, knowing how interested he was in calendars, we tried asking him subtraction questions that incorporated problems about calendar dates.

This alteration produced a huge positive effect. He now answered each of a long list of questions correctly, producing the answers quickly and easily. In addition to finding it easy to solve problems that were formally similar to the previous ones (for example, "If a girl was born in 1904, how old would she have been in 1926?"), he could also do much harder subtraction problems, such as "If a man was born in 1879, how old would he have been in 1924?".

We tend to assume that a person's level of competence at any kind of ability remains at a certain level unless it is altered by positive influences such as training or practice, or negative ones such as boredom or tiredness. The findings reported in this chapter challenge that assumption. Take the case of the boy who could solve calendar date problems, for instance. Had we simply used a standard arithmetic test to assess the boy's capacity to subtract, it would have been concluded that he had a very low level of ability. Yet that conclusion would have been quite wrong, as was evident from the boy's good performance when he was given subtraction problems that were presented in a different way. Once again, the research findings demonstrate that a person's ability levels may be far from being fixed or constant.

Even in people of normal intelligence, the ability to solve arithmetic problems can be strongly affected by the way in which the tasks are presented. In a study that was carried out in Liberia by researcher Jean Lave (1977), some men who worked as tailors were given arithmetic questions to solve. The questions were presented either in the guise of tailoring problems (involving measurements used in working with cloth) or in the form of typical school tasks. Even when the formal arithmetic needed in order to solve a problem was identical in the two situations, the tailors did far better if a problem was described in a tailoring context than if it was presented as a school task. What is more, the best predictor of their success at the tailoring problems was the person's number of years of experience as a tailor. But when formally identical arithmetic problems were presented as school tasks rather than tailoring ones, the reverse applied. Here the best predictor of a person's success was the number of years of schooling the person had received.

These results provide yet more evidence that assessments of someone's ability level can be strongly affected by the context in which a problem is posed. Additional indications that levels of competence in individuals may be fluid rather than fixed have emerged from research

conducted among "street children" in Brazil. Some of these children make a living by selling lottery tickets (Schliemann, 1988). In order to be able to buy and sell lottery tickets successfully, these children have gained a sophisticated understanding of mathematical probabilities. But if they are given school-type problems that involve the very same probability skills as the ones they use when dealing in tickets, the children cannot do them at all. Conversely, students who have learned about probability at school do far worse than the street children when given tasks in which they have to apply their knowledge in non-school contexts. Once again, it is clear that a young person's ability to solve formally identical problems greatly depends on the particular context in which the problems are presented.

Child street vendor in Brazil. Photograph courtesy TRIP, photographer S.Grant

How a problem is displayed

Contextual effects on skilled performance can be just as large in other areas of skill as they are in arithmetic. In one investigation, for instance, the researchers assessed children's ability to estimate the movements of objects on a video screen (Ceci, 1990). As in the other studies, in each of two conditions the task was formally identical, and only the manner in which the situation was portrayed was different. In both conditions children saw objects shown on a video screen. They had to predict where each object would move to next. They did this by using a joystick to move a cross on the screen. Each object was one of three different shapes, two colours and two sizes. Thus there were 12 possible combinations of object features. Their movement was governed by various rules, such as squares go up, circles go down, dark objects move right, light objects move left, large objects move in one direction, and small objects in the opposite direction.

By combining these rules, the children could predict, at least in principle, the future movement of any kind of object, such as a large red square. However, they did not succeed at learning the rules that dictated the movements of each kind of objects and applying this knowledge to make accurate predictions. Even after fifteen 50-trial sessions they were still performing at little better than chance level.

In the other condition the children had essentially the same task to perform, but the way in which it was explained to them was very different. These youngsters were told that they were playing a video game. The objects on the screen were the same colours and sizes as the ones in the other condition, but they were altered from squares, circles, and triangles to butterflies, bumblebees, and birds. The children who participated in this condition were not just asked to place a cross on the part of the screen where they thought the object would move to, but were told that they were to "capture the prey". As in the other condition, they made their response by moving the joystick, but they were told that by doing this they were taking a "butterfly net" to the designated location.

Although these alterations only affected the manner in which the task was presented to the participants, and left the actual nature of the task itself unchanged, they had a large influence on performance levels. Those children who were assigned to the second condition easily outperformed the other subjects: the former had near-perfect scores. Once again, the outcome was that assessments of abilities to perform a task were greatly affected by the differing contexts in which the task was presented. And once more, the findings challenge the view that a person's abilities are fixed quantities.

To what extent are a person's different abilities independent of one another?

The boy who could solve difficult calendar date problems despite being mentally handicapped had a very uneven profile of mental abilities. He was unusually competent in one area of expertise at the same time as being defective in others. Most people find this surprising. We tend to assume that although we are more capable in some spheres of ability than in others, there is a degree of uniformity. We expect people to be broadly similar in their level of ability to perform different kinds of mental tasks. The fact that there exist mentally handicapped "savants" in whom this is clearly not true raises the possibility that even ordinary people's different abilities may be more independent of one another than they are often assumed to be. Perhaps different abilities are not linked to each other, except in particular circumstances.

As we discovered in the previous section, even within narrow skill areas there may large differences in a person's level of performance at a problem when the task circumstances are altered. This finding encourages one to expect that a person's different abilities may be somewhat distinct, and separate from one another. On the whole, research findings confirm this view. That is to say, the fact that someone is well qualified in one sphere of ability does not necessarily lead to their doing well at tasks requiring another capability, even when the two abilities are similar. Only to a limited extent do a person's different abilities influence each other. So being a good chess player certainly does not make it easier for someone to learn an unfamiliar modern language, and may not even affect the acquisition of skills that appear to be more similar to chess.

There is plenty of anecdotal evidence that particular skills can be fragmentary and set apart from other abilities. Numerous findings demonstrate that a person can be simultaneously average in one sphere of ability and below average in another, even when the abilities concerned are apparently quite similar. One person to remark on this was the famous mathematician Norbert Wiener, who wrote an autobiographical account of his childhood (Wiener, 1953). He was a very clever child, and regarded as a prodigy, but although the young Norbert was certainly precocious in some areas of knowledge, he was not at all advanced in others. In his autobiography, he recalled that until the age of 7 he still believed in Santa Claus, despite the fact that by that time he was already reading difficult books about science.

A further indication that children's different abilities can be fragmentary and unrelated was provided by Francis Galton, who was a cousin of Charles Darwin and the founding father of research into intelligence. Galton recalled that at the age of 8 he too was considered to be an unusually bright child. All the same, at that age he wondered how some Latin school books he discovered in a cupboard could have stayed fresh and clean through the 2000 year period since Roman times. He had naively assumed that any book by a Roman author must be that old.

Even within the same general area of ability, a person who is good at some of the skills that contribute to it will not necessarily be above average at the other component skills. For instance, in the area of musical ability there are many different sub-skills that contribute to a person's competence as a musician, and it is entirely possible for a person to be excellent at some of them but poor at others (Sloboda, 1985). One individual may be superb at sight-reading but a relatively indifferent player by ear, for example.

What is more, even within what seems to be one unitary ability, such as memory, there can be large differences in a single person's levels of competence at different kinds of challenges. This has been shown when people have been assessed at a number of different memory tests. Doing this makes it possible to discover to what extent someone who does well at one memory test will also do well at another one. It turns out that the correlations between the same individuals' performance levels at the different memory tests are only a little above zero. In other words, someone who does well at one memory test is no more likely than anyone else to perform well at a different memory test. This finding challenges the widespread assumption that most people tend to do either well or not so well at memory challenges in general, and can be regarded as having good memories or bad memories. Contrary to what many people believe, the extent to which a person does well at a memory task is highly specific to that particular task.

Why are performance levels correlated?

It remains true that there is a tendency for people who do well at one kind of mental challenge to also do well at other mental tasks: at school, for instance, young people who do well at maths exams tend to do well in other subjects too. But why should this happen if a person's different abilities really are as independent and separate as has been claimed in this section? There are three possible reasons:

- The first is that any two tasks, even in different areas of ability, may involve certain skills in common. For instance, solving problems of many kinds may depend on a person's number skills, and for that reason someone with good number skills will find them helpful in a variety of different situations.
- Second, with two different tasks it is sometimes the case that there are items of knowledge that are relevant to both of them. This provides another reason why there is a tendency for a person's level of performance at different tasks to be correlated.
- Third, even in circumstances in which two tasks or problems have nothing at all in common, there are certain qualities of the person who is attempting them that will have a similar influence on performance at both tasks. For instance, someone who is unusually self-confident, or especially attentive, or good at persevering when things get difficult, or unusually motivated to do well, will be helped by these qualities in a range of task situations, even when the abilities that are called upon are very different. Similarly, being depressed, pessimistic, or easily distracted and poor at concentrating, will handicap a person in a range of different situations.

These three reasons all contribute to the fact that people who do well in one sphere of ability tend to do well at different kinds of mental tasks. As we have seen, although this finding may appear to suggest that a person's different abilities are connected rather than being truly separate, that is not necessarily the case.

Do abilities transfer?

A common belief is that there is considerable "transfer" between different abilities, and that this occurs not only when they have identical elements. For example, it is often claimed that someone who learns classical languages thereby acquires the capacity to think clearly. The finding that each of a person's specific abilities may actually be more separate and independent of the same person's other abilities than is usually assumed, raises the possibility that this claim may be in need of revision.

To what extent, and in what circumstances, do particular capabilities actually transfer or generalise, making it easier for the learner to acquire other similar skills? In what circumstances can capabilities that a person has gained be applied in situations that are very different from those in which they were first acquired? A likely consequence of the finding that even the narrowest skills and abilities are largely independent of one another is that "transfer of training" is restricted. Perhaps such transfer is limited to situations where the different tasks contain elements that are identical. Research findings confirm this suggestion, showing that the degree to which new skills transfer or generalise is indeed very limited.

Consider, for instance, the findings of an investigation by Chase and Ericsson (1981). Over a two-year period they followed the progress of a young man who engaged in large amounts of practice at a memory task. It involved listening to, and then immediately attempting to recall, lists made up of random digits that had been presented at a rate of one item per second. At the beginning of the training period the individual's performance at this task was no better than average. His "digit span" (the longest list he could recall without error) was around eight items. But with the greatly extended training he was given, his performance improved considerably. Eventually he was able to recall lists containing as many as 80 digits.

This is certainly an impressive demonstration that a memory skill can be greatly improved by training. Yet the practical value to the individual of his newly acquired skill was somewhat limited. This became apparent whenever he tried to remember lists of items other than digits, such as letters or words. Disappointingly, it was found that in spite of the fact that the man's memory for digits had dramatically increased, his ability to remember other kinds of information hardly changed at all. He was still no better than the average person at recalling items such as letters and words. It appears that the young man's newly gained skill was a very narrow and specific one. This new expertise did not generalise or transfer to tasks that involved remembering items other than the digit materials on which he had been trained. All that had changed was his memory for digits. Despite all the training he had received, his memory in general had not improved at all.

Of course, the finding that transfer of training to different tasks and problems does not always occur (even when people are given tasks that involve very similar skills to the trained ones) does not mean that transfer of training *never* takes place. However, research findings show that transfer occurs only in particular circumstances. It can never be taken for granted that someone who has acquired a certain kind of expertise will automatically be able to extend what has been gained to new situations, or to problems that were not encountered during training.

Generally speaking, in order for a person to be able to apply a newly gained skill or ability to novel tasks or problems that have not been met previously, it is necessary for there to be elements in common between the new task or problem and those specific skills on which the person has been trained. The common elements should be virtually identical: mere similarity may not be enough. And even when common elements do exist, that alone may not be enough to guarantee transfer. Some further encouragement may be needed in order for a person to become flexible and confident enough to apply newly gained knowledge, or a new skill, in circumstances that are at all different from those in which the skill was acquired.

Do specific abilities depend on general intelligence?

Some of the findings that have been described in this chapter suggest that even within the same broad area of ability, such as music or memory, each specific skill may have a distinctly "stand-alone" quality. That is, the different skills, even when they are similar, may be independent of one another to a considerable extent. As we have seen, an important practical consequence of this is to limit the degree to which transfer of training takes place between different acquired capabilities.

In this section we ask about the extent to which a person's particular capabilities depend on that individual's general level of ability. For example, in what circumstances is it the case that in order to gain certain skills someone has to have considerable general intellectual ability, or "intelligence", as indicated by a high IQ test score?

Within psychology, there is some disagreement on this question. One view is that there are certain broad underlying abilities that must be present in a person in order for other capabilities to be acquired. In particular, it has been suggested that general intellectual ability "underlies" those capabilities that are more specific. If this is true, it will normally be impossible for someone whose general ability is limited to acquire certain intellectual skills, especially ones that involve complex or abstract thinking. However, some other psychologists have challenged that account. They are not convinced that general intelligence or any other broader abilities should necessarily be regarded as underlying more specific ones, or as being more basic or less changeable.

One way of shedding light on the issue is by measuring the relationships, or correlations, between intelligence-test scores and performance at various tasks that use the particular kinds of knowledge and skills a person has acquired. Generally speaking, positive correlations are the rule. This is not a surprising finding, considering that the test items that make up an intelligence test are chosen partly in order to sample people's intellectual capabilities. The correlations between measures of tested general intelligence and indications of a person's ability to do particular things are often fairly low, however. For instance, correlations between intelligence test (IQ) scores and measures of employees' performance at jobs are usually found to be low, typically around +.2 to +.4.

Correlations of this low magnitude account for no more than around 15% of the variability in people's job performance. This is because in order to estimate the extent to which knowing the value of one factor (or "variable") helps to predict the other one that is correlated with it, one simply squares the correlation. Thus, knowing how well someone did at an IQ test improves our capacity to predict how someone performs their job by between +.2 squared (.04, or 4%) and +.4 squared, or 16%. It is clear from this example that when the correlation between two measures is a modest one, only to a limited extent does this provide a basis for making better-than-chance estimates.

Perhaps surprisingly, it is not hard to find instances in which a person's level of success at particular problems, even ones that seem to demand considerable intelligence, may be entirely unrelated to their intelligence test scores. We have already seen, for instance, that some mentally handicapped individuals who do poorly at intelligence tests can nevertheless perform difficult mental feats. Some of these

"savants", like the boy described earlier, are good at calendar problems. Others excel at mental arithmetic or do remarkable feats of memory. A few have remarkable musical or artistic abilities.

These demonstrations that there are mentally handicapped people who can solve problems that are thought to require intelligence raise the possibility that the links between general intelligence and specific abilities are actually rather weak. Other research findings show that even in people of average intelligence their capacity to do difficult problems need not be at all closely related to their intelligence levels.

In one investigation (Ceci & Liker, 1986) race-track gamblers were given detailed information about horses entered in imaginary races, and asked to predict the odds on each horse winning. To solve these problems, each horse's real speed and strength has to be estimated after making allowances for all the factors that could have affected performances at previous races. This is a difficult task, because in order to estimate the odds accurately various items of information have to be considered. These include data on the state of the racecourse, and details of the horses' previous performances, including previous race positions and times, and also detailed evidence of other factors that could have affected success. To make the task even more difficult, it is not just a matter of adding up the combined influences of all the

Drawings by an autistic child, Nadia (left), and an average 6.5 year old child. Nadia lacked language and her gross motor development was very retarded but she produced exquisite drawings from memory (Reproduced by permission from L. Selfe (1976). An autistic child with exceptional drawing ability. In G.E. Butterworh (Ed.), *The child's representation of the world*. New York: Plenum Publishing different factors that could have affected a horse's previous success, because the different influences interact with one another. So it is impossible for someone to succeed at these handicapping problems unless they can do some complicated kinds of reasoning.

The problems were given to a number of male gamblers and racing enthusiasts who were knowledgeable about horse-racing. Some of them did much better than others. The researchers had previously measured their intelligence. By correlating the men's IQ scores with their performance levels at the problems, it was possible to assess the extent to which performance was related to measured intelligence.

The correlation was found to be zero. In other words, there was no relationship at all between a person's IQ score and how well that person did at the horseracing problems. Some individuals with very low IQ scores did much better than some men who not only had high IQs but also possessed university degrees and professional qualifications. This finding clearly shows that, in these circumstances, the capacity to do well at a cognitively complex and difficult task was unrelated to the kind of intelligence that is assessed in an IQ test.

A number of additional situations have come to light in which expertise at demanding mental problems seems not to be related to general intelligence. In one study, for instance, it was found that dairy workers developed complicated mental strategies that avoided energy being wasted by lifting and moving heavy objects (Scribner, 1984). Reaching the most effective decisions required some fairly complicated mental operations, and yet it was found that the workers' success at making those decisions was unrelated to their intelligence test scores. In yet another study, by a German research team headed by D. Dörner (see Ceci, 1990), people had to imagine they were managing a small city, and had to make decisions that involved taking into account a large number of competing factors. Once again, it was found that degree of success at this demanding task was not related to participants' formal education or intelligence.

Are some abilities unchangeable?

Because certain abilities are broader than others, or involve a combination of different skills and various kinds of knowledge, we might expect them to be more stable than others, and perhaps harder to change. Take the skills that are assessed in an intelligence test, for example. When individuals' intelligence is tested on a number of separate occasions their scores tend to remain fairly stable. This could mean that IQ scores are essentially unchangeable, except to a small degree. However, there is evidence that in certain circumstances a person's IQ score can change very considerably.

First, studies of adoption provide one source of findings demonstrating large changes in IQ. A number of investigations have found that the average IQs of children from poor families who are adopted early in life by adults who are able to provide a stimulating and supportive home environment can be as much as 20 points higher than those of either their biological parents or of brothers and sisters brought up by the biological parents (see Howe, 1997). These results strongly suggest that even as broad and fundamental an ability as general intelligence can be substantially altered, when children are placed in an environment that provides them with plenty of encouragement and good opportunities to learn.

Second, as we discovered in Chapter 2, further evidence that IQ levels can change, sometimes substantially, has emerged from a substantial number of educational intervention programmes. These were designed to provide special learning opportunities for young children whose home environments have failed to provide the kinds of support and encouragement in which children's abilities thrive. In a number of cases there has been considerable success in raising young children's IQ levels. Critics of these programmes have noted that in some instances the gains have faded after some years. However, this has only happened when there has been a failure to continue providing the educational opportunities that children need. In some cases the improvements have been small, but that has usually been because the duration and intensity of the programme has been insufficient.

Third, a number of studies have shown that intelligence levels are affected by schooling. For instance:

- Investigations of the influence of the summer vacation on IQ scores have shown decreases during the summer vacation months. The largest decreases have been found in those young people whose summer activities have been most dissimilar to those associated with school (Ceci, 1990).
- A Swedish investigation by K. Harnquist (cited in Ceci, 1990) studied the outcomes of dropping out of school. Among boys whose IQ, socioeconomic status, and school grades were equivalent before they dropped out, there was a loss of 1.8 IQ points on average for each year of school that was missed.
- Other studies conducted in remote American communities in the 1930s, where schools sometimes closed down for short or

longer periods, have shown advantages of 10–30 points for those children who had the most schooling compared with those who had the least. In one community, children born in 1940, who had adequate schooling, had IQs on average 11 points higher than children born in 1930, whose schooling was interrupted (see Ceci, 1990).

- Similarly, in a study conducted in South Africa to examine the consequences of schooling being delayed or cut short for reasons outside the family's control, it was discovered that the sooner a child's schooling began, and the greater the duration of schooling, the higher the children's IQ scores (Schmidt, 1966).

- In yet another investigation the researchers took advantage of the fact that children in the German school system had to be 6 years old by April 1st on the year of entering school. So children whose birthdays were around that date could have up to a year's difference in schooling despite being of a very similar age. The researchers discovered that 8-year-olds who had more schooling than most were close in mental abilities to those 10-year-olds who had received the least schooling, and well ahead of 8-year-olds who, because of their birth dates, had started school late (Baltes & Reinert, 1969).

Taken together, the research findings do not support the view that certain abilities are unchangeable. In the right circumstances, even the mental abilities assessed in an intelligence test can and do change substantially.

Summary

Human abilities are extremely varied: they can be broad or narrow, and there is no agreed answer to the question of how many abilities people possess. Abilities are often fluid rather than fixed: the degree to which someone succeeds at a challenge can be greatly influenced by factors such as time and place, the individual's mental state, the personal significance of the task, and the manner in which the problem is displayed.

To a considerable extent one person's different abilities can each be highly separate, and independent of the same person's other abilities. The degree to which particular abilities transfer or generalise is restricted. On the whole, specific abilities are largely independent of the person's general level of intellectual ability, or intelligence. People whose intelligence test scores are low may nevertheless be capable of success at solving difficult problems that demand complex or abstract thinking.

Although it has been claimed that certain abilities may be largely unchangeable, research findings show that even the mental abilities assessed in an intelligence test can alter substantially.

Further reading

Some fascinating research demonstrating the effects of context on human abilities is described in S.J. Ceci (1990), *On intelligence ... more or less: A bio-ecological treatise on intellectual development* (Englewood Cliffs, NJ: Prentice Hall).

The relationship between particular abilities and general intelligence is discussed in M.J.A. Howe (1997), *IQ in question: The truth about intelligence* (London: Sage).

The role of motivation 4

I n Chapter 1 we discovered that learning takes place as a direct end-product of the mental processing activities a person undertakes. Now we turn to some of the influences that affect learning indirectly, by making those mental activities happen. Each of these broader influences has large effects on what people actually learn, both at school and in everyday life.

The importance of the various indirect influences were highlighted a generation ago in an influential book about schools, entitled *How children fail* (Holt, 1964). That book demonstrated that many children were failing to thrive as classroom learners, not because they lacked intelligence or the capacity to learn, or because the quality of the instruction was inadequate, but for reasons that were connected to their emotions and feelings (Holt, 1964). The author, a teacher named John Holt, observed that many pupils were chronically anxious, fearful of failing, and worried about teachers' reactions to their work. As a result, the children were too concerned about getting right answers and avoiding trouble, and not self-confident enough to be thoughtful and imaginative in the classroom. This was despite the fact that most of the children Holt observed came from loving and supportive homes and attended good schools. If even these fortunate children were too fearful and anxious to do as well as they should have done, other children whose home and school circumstances were not so good must have been experiencing more serious problems, Holt concluded.

Indirect influences on learning: Attention, motivation, and study habits

Some of the most essential influences on everyday learning are ones that we might fail to notice if our awareness of learning depended entirely on knowing about experimental studies such as the ones described in Chapter 1. Psychological experiments typically take place over periods of minutes or hours, but in real life the acquisition of

capabilities is likely to take much lengthier periods of time. In these circumstances, ensuring that learning activities are maintained requires special provisions that would not be necessary if all learning took place in brief episodes.

In this chapter we shall encounter three kinds of influences that have especially important effects on children's learning. The first influence is identified by noting that (1) It is essential that people *attend to* learning tasks. In everyday life, paying attention and maintaining sustained concentration are crucial ingredients of learning. Children and adults who are too impulsive or distractible do not thrive as learners. To be an effective learner, a person has to attend carefully and persist even when there are distractions that may be hard to resist. It is not always easy to concentrate on tasks and keep paying attention, however. So learners need to have reasons for doing so. This is especially important with those skills that take a long time to master.

The second source of influences on learning is suggested by the observation that for a person to keep attending throughout all this time, there do have to be good incentives. In other words (2) Learners need to be strongly *motivated* to keep attending to the task.

As was remarked in Chapter 1, if we think of learning as being like a manufacturing process, motivation provides the fuel that makes the process happen. Motivation affects human learning in a number of ways, with differences between people in how they are motivated forming a major reason why individuals vary so much in the abilities they gain. For example, a key reason for the finding that many Norwegians speak English although few English people understand any Norwegian, is that there are more incentives for a Norwegian person to learn English than for an English person to study Norwegian. In common with other learned accomplishments such as mastering a musical instrument, acquiring a foreign language takes a lot of hard work, and there have to be solid justifications for making the effort.

Motivation plays an enormous part in the acquisition of human abilities, and we shall examine its contribution to learning in the present chapter. We shall look at some of the ways in which motivation affects the kinds of learning activities people engage in. This, in turn, determines the varieties of learned qualities, skills, and abilities they acquire. As we shall see, there are many different motives for learning. In practice, motivational influences are often intertwined with individuals' personal characteristics, such as personality and temperament, which make important contributions to learning. For instance, the kinds of learning activities someone undertakes can be influenced by various personal attributes, including the person's self-confidence, optimism, and competitiveness.

In addition, certain kinds of learning, especially ones that require prolonged concentration, become easier, and consequently more likely to occur, when a person has got into the habit of regularly spending time on particular tasks. Habits form a third kind of influence on learning. As a rule (3) By establishing good working habits or *study habits* people make themselves into productive learners.

All three of these influences are examined in the present chapter. First, we look at some of the ways in which attending and concentrating contribute to human learning and the acquisition of abilities. Second, we consider some of the most important motivational influences, and observe various ways in which motivation, temperament, and personality combine to affect people's achievements as learners. Third the chapter will examine some of the factors that can help a person to acquire some of the study habits that provide the other important source of indirect influences on the acquisition of abilities.

For the sake of simplicity we shall consider the various influences one at a time. In practice, however, they all operate in conjunction with one another, and merge together. For instance, some of the topics we shall be examining, such as "perceived locus of control" and "fear of failure" are in effect compounds that include elements of motivation, personality, and temperament. They are also related to a person's study habits and capacity to attend or concentrate.

It is important to remember that although the kinds of influences on learning that are examined in the present chapter do not act quite so directly as the mental activities and processes that were described in Chapter 1, they are nevertheless just as crucial, especially in the long run. Children and adults cannot gain abilities unless they carry out the kinds of mental processing activities that produce learning, but it is equally true that there have to be incentives in order for a person to keep on engaging in those mental activities.

Attending

We start with the activity of attending. When speculating about the reasons why one individual is better informed than someone else, or has more skills, people often assume that the causes must lie deep within the individuals concerned. Perhaps the first individual has more underlying general ability, or higher intelligence, or some special innate potential to do well. However, mundane differences can be just as important, and differences between people in what they learn can have a variety of different causes. One that is particularly important but is often overlooked, perhaps because it seems so obvious and ordinary, is that some people simply direct their attention more effectively than others.

Attending behaviours have an enormous effect on how and when and what a person learns. This is demonstrated by the findings of a number of studies in which people were encouraged to attend to different aspects of various events that they saw. In one investigation, for instance, participants were asked to spend a minute looking at a coloured magazine picture (Bransford, Nitsch, & Franks, 1977). Some people were told to look carefully for some small xs that were drawn on the picture. Others were told to look at the actual objects in the picture. Later, when the participants were unexpectedly asked to try to recall the objects that had appeared in the picture, it was found that those individuals who were told to concentrate on the objects were able to remember as much as seven times as many objects as the other participants.

Attending in the classroom

The Bransford et al. experiment illustrates the fact that, as is recognised whenever an exasperated teacher complains to his or her pupils "You aren't listening to what I'm saying", those mental activities that produce learning only occur if someone is attending appropriately. That is particularly important in the school classroom. For example, 10-year-old Harry is bright and curious, but in the classroom he is easily distracted and finds it hard to concentrate; so he fails to hear much of the information provided by the teacher. Research in schools has confirmed that those children who — unlike Harry — spend a high proportion of their time carefully attending to classroom tasks, learn far more than children who do not. As a result, those children who are good at concentrating are more successful than pupils like Harry, who are more easily distracted.

It is not the sheer amount of attending that is most important. What matters most is attending to the right things. For instance, in a school classroom, where it can be very important to listen closely to what the teacher is saying, a young child will be at a disadvantage if she has failed to gain the habit of listening. That can happen all too easily, perhaps because of a lack of opportunities at home to have the kinds of regular conversations with parents or other adults that make a young person experienced in listening carefully to what other people say. Not all young children will spontaneously direct all their attention to those elements of classroom life that the teacher regards as being most important. Some youngsters, such as Harry, need a fair amount of help and encouragement in order to get into the habit of carefully attending to the teacher's words.

However, in identifying defective attending as a learning problem we should be careful not to jump to the conclusion that any young child who is poor at attending in the classroom must be suffering from a permanent handicap or disorder. When things go wrong it is all to easy to give the complaint a label and rush to the conclusion that some underlying pathological condition is the cause of the problems. With children who are not good at attending, for example, there is a temptation to assume that such a child is being held back by a trait of "impulsivity" or "distractibility" that makes concentrating impossible. But in the majority of cases that is not so. This is shown by the fact that the very same child whose classroom behaviour seems to indicate a total inability to concentrate may be perfectly capable of maintaining attention to a game he or she really enjoys or a favourite television show. In Harry's case, for instance, as soon as he is out of the classroom and on the school playground enjoying a game of football, anyone can see that his mind is totally concentrated on what he is doing. This demonstrates that Harry's basic powers of attending and concentrating are perfectly sound.

Attending, like most kinds of behaviour, is itself greatly influenced by acquired skills and habits. So when a child or an adult is handicapped by a failure to concentrate on learning tasks, instead of simply labelling the person as impulsive or distractible, it is much more helpful to look for opportunities to help the person to gain those attending skills that are lacking. Rather than assuming that there must be something fundamentally wrong with a child who has difficulty concentrating, a more realistic response is to observe that for one reason or another the child has not yet gained attending skills and habits that are necessary in order for young people to make the best of their capacities as learners. Expressing the problem in that way reminds us that remedies can be found in the majority of cases.

Teachers in Japanese schools are often particularly effective at helping children to become good at concentrating on tasks. That is partly because the teachers are made aware of the fact that their pupils may need help with attending. Consequently, teachers place emphasis on encouraging young children to learn to attend and concentrate in the classroom, with very positive results (Stevenson & Stigler, 1993). Children in Japan who master difficult accomplishments often owe part of their success to having had the habit of carefully attending to instructions instilled during childhood.

Varieties of motivation

Attending helps to make learning possible because it creates a state of affairs in which the active mental processing that produces learning is most likely take place. But what makes learners attend in the first place? In order to gain practical insights into the causes of learning in real life, we not only have to examine learning activities and processes that take place when a person attends to new events or information, as we did in Chapter 1, but we must also go a step further back and discover what makes learners attend.

As was noted earlier, in order for someone to attend in the appropriate manner, there needs to be a reason or incentive for doing just that. This leads to yet another question, "What are some of the incentives that help a person to attend to or concentrate on a task?". Trying to provide an answer brings us to the topic of motivation. By and large, children and adults attend to events and happenings when they are motivated to do so.

Motives and incentives provide the reasons for someone behaving in one way rather than another, or deciding whether or not to attend to a perceived event or concentrate on a task. In certain non-human species motivation is based on a relatively small number of needs or drives, with rewards acting as *reinforcers* that increase the likelihood of the behaviour preceding them being repeated. Humans, in contrast, can be motivated in many different ways.

There are numerous kinds of human motives. Among the first that come to mind are financial rewards, desire for success, curiosity, and the need for approval. Motivational influences do not operate in a vacuum. Their effectiveness often depends on characteristics of the individual person, including age, intelligence, temperament, and personality. In the following section we examine some of the ways in which motivational influences can affect the likelihood of a person gaining needed skills and abilities. We shall discover how individuals' personalities and temperaments can work together with motivation to affect learning. As well as positive influences, some negative motivational influences that can hinder learning will be discussed, and we shall consider how to circumvent them.

Extrinsic and intrinsic motivation

If you pay someone to listen carefully to everything you say they will probably do just that, so long as the price is right. Money provides an external or *extrinsic* reward for an activity. In contrast, internal or *intrinsic* rewards are more closely connected to the activity itself. Such rewards include interest in the task itself and the enjoyment that a person gets from doing something out of a sense of curiosity. Quite often an activity is both intrinsically and extrinsically motivated, as when people work at improving a skill partly because they enjoy it and partly because they enjoy the success it brings.

It is often asserted that the most effective kind of learning is learning for its own sake, and up to a point that is true. But there is nothing inherently wrong with extrinsic motivation, and it is especially valuable at the early stages of an activity. This is one reason why parents are advised to give plenty of praise for their young children's efforts to learn. At early stages of learning, especially when children and young people are faced with entirely new and difficult challenges, they need all the help they can get. The support of an adult who is generous with praise and encouragement may make all the difference in helping a young person to begin making progress towards gaining expertise at tasks that may at first seem dauntingly difficult.

However, sometimes external rewards can get in the way of a person enjoying an activity for its own sake. When this happens, such rewards may clash with the benefits that come from intrinsic motivation. That is especially likely when internal motivation is already high. Here, external rewards may in some circumstances not only be unhelpful but actually interfere with learning.

Negative outcomes of rewards were observed in an investigation in which nursery school children were given rewards for engaging in play activities that they already enjoyed. The children who participated had been assigned to different groups. One group were told that if they continued to play with the felt-pens and drawing materials they had already been playing with they would be given a "Good Player" certificate. The outcome was to make them less active and creative (Lepper, Green, & Nisbett, 1973). Other groups of children were not given this information, but were simply allowed to play with the materials. During the session in which they were observed these children spent twice as much time drawing as the children in the first group.

There have been similar findings in other studies. For instance, in a series of experiments conducted by Teresa Amabile (1983) it was discovered that when children's paintings were regularly praised by teachers, the contents of the artwork tended to become progressively more conventional and less original or creative.

These findings demonstrate that there is much to be said for learning that is strongly motivated by a person's interest in the task, rather than by external rewards. Only then can the learner be said to be genuinely independent of other people. When the effort to learn is being maintained largely because of external incentives, whether these involve payment, prestige, or the possibility of getting other people's approval, there is always the possibility that as soon as these are taken away learning will decrease or even cease.

Balancing internal and external rewards. Learners who are sustained largely by their own interests do seem to be more independent, and better able to function effectively on their own. This has important consequences. High levels of intrinsic motivation are characteristic of learners who are mature and truly independent. At school, a pupil who is used to getting plenty of attention and praise may function perfectly well as a learner. But after leaving school, if that person has become too dependent on those kinds of external supports he or she may be reluctant to take up new learning challenges, simply because the old incentives are not longer present. So by and large it makes sense to encourage learners to be motivated less by "extrinsic" (external) factors, like praise, approval, and financial rewards, and more by internal or "intrinsic" ones that are closely connected to whatever is being learned.

However, it would be a mistake to push that reasoning too far. Extrinsic motivation is not necessarily always inferior to intrinsic motivation; and it is not true that mature individuals never need external rewards. In the real world almost everyone does, to some extent. Even among geniuses, who are some of the most experienced and successful learners of all, it is common to find that incentives such as fame, fortune, and the wish for prestige are not entirely absent from their minds. Of course, these individuals' levels of intrinsic motivation — in the form of their sheer interest in what they are trying to do — are extremely high, and without the driving power of this interest and the sense of direction that it helps to produce, it is unlikely that anyone would ever attain great creative achievements. But all the same, even the most creative people sometimes benefit from having external incentives as well.

So there are reasons for not being too eager to downgrade the contribution of extrinsic motivation. And as we have seen, although it is true that intrinsic motivation may eventually come to play a big role in sustaining a person's learning or study activities, in the early stages of learning something new and unfamiliar it is unlikely that internal motivation, on its own, will be enough to provide adequate incentives. Often, it is only when a certain level of competence has already been reached that an activity becomes interesting for its own sake. Especially for a young and immature learner, praise and encouragement may do much to help

an individual reach that stage. For example, young children learning to play a musical instrument invariably need plenty of support. One reason is that, especially in the early stages, until some basic instrumental skills have been gained, progress is bound to be slow. Another is that learning activities such as solitary practising and rehearsing scales are not intrinsically motivating for young children. Because of that, until there exists enough intrinsic motivation to maintain the child's concentration, external rewards and incentives may be crucial.

Photograph courtesy TRIP

However, in most areas of ability there eventually comes a time when young learners who have remained dependent on external rewards and the constant encouragement of adults and have failed to learn to find satisfaction within the activity itself, will be at a real disadvantage. These learners will be unable to compete with individuals who are more self-directed and independent.

Up to a point, the more reasons a person has for doing something, the more likely it is to be done. This is especially true for those tasks and challenges that are especially arduous or daunting. The fact that there exist various different kinds of motivation is one reflection of the fact that people have many different needs. There are obvious gains to be made by engaging in a learning experience that will help meet several of a person's needs rather than just one.

Positive motivational influences: 1. Achievement motivation

As everyone knows, performance at many kinds of tasks is affected by the extent to which a person desires to do well. This source of influence has been systematically investigated in research that began with some studies undertaken by a psychologist named David McClelland, who investigated *achievement motivation* (McClelland, 1978). He introduced that term to refer to the desire to perform well and reach high standards.

Up to a point it is true to say that *everyone* wants to do well and strives to achieve. Yet people vary in the extent to which this is so. Measures of people's differing achievement motivation provide useful predictions of future success, even when their intelligence levels are equivalent. Individuals differ in achievement motivation from early childhood. Children who strive hard to succeed tend to become adults whose levels of achievement motivation remain high. Differences between people in the level of their achievement motivation are largely acquired, with the contribution of inheritance being fairly small.

The German social theorist Max Weber demonstrated that the stress on individual success and competitiveness that is taken for granted in Western culture is to some extent a product of protestant values and the capitalist way of life that replaced medieval feudalism. Because the social structures of feudal societies were largely static, for most people in those days the idea that by striving hard they could better themselves and acquire wealth or power would have been unrealistic. Even now, of course, there are large differences between different societies in the extent to which people believe it is realistically possible that their own efforts will produce desirable changes in their lives. And even in the Western democracies, although competition and the desire for individual success are widely encouraged, there are some sub-cultures in which very different values are stressed. For all these reasons, there are large differences between individuals in their levels of achievement motivation.

There are many factors that bear upon an individual's level of achievement motivation. A child's family background is one important influence:

- Achievement motivation tends to be high in those young people who have been encouraged to gain the skills that make a person independent.
- Youngsters are especially likely to have high levels of achievement motivation if they have parents who encourage their children to be outgoing and self-reliant, to make friends with other children, to try hard without constantly asking for help, and to find their way around and do things for themselves.
- Children whose parents are more restrictive and do not encourage them to play with other young people or make their own decisions tend to be lower in achievement motivation.
- Other parental actions that are associated

Tree-house dwellers protesting the route of the M11 link road; environmental activists using their lifestyle to influence public opinion. Photograph courtesy TRIP, photographer H. Roberts

with high levels of achievement motivation in their children include demonstrating warmth, having high expectations, and giving plenty of rewards and encouragement.

However, encouraging independence and having high expectations can sometimes have negative consequences. This is especially likely when parents are negligent or too casual in their approach to their child, or fail to give enough support. Those children whose parents expect them to be independent and self-reliant when they are very young, and yet do not provide needed help and do not reward their child's successes, or are too inclined to criticise the child's failures, are likely to become anxious about failing. As a result, these children may get into the habit of avoiding difficult challenges.

So in order for a child to be motivated to strive and succeed it is certainly important that the parents encourage independence and self-reliance, but it is equally necessary to provide a relatively democratic and non-authoritarian environment. The child needs to be given plenty of support, warmth, and affection, with little or no pressure to succeed, and an absence of criticism or disapproval on those inevitable occasions when the child fails at a particular task. In short, for achievement motivation to be an entirely positive force it is necessary for a young person to have experienced a *combination* of:

- encouragement for independence; and
- plenty of support and help.

Also, when early failures have unpleasant consequences, such as humiliation or shame, the chances are that rather than seeking new challenges the child will steer clear of tasks in which failing seems at all likely.

Positive motivational influences: 2. Internal locus of control

People differ from one another in the way in which they perceive the causes of their successes and failures. Some young people think that how well they do is largely out of their hands, and depends on various external factors, including luck, innate talents, fate, and the influence of other people. Others appreciate that what they can achieve and the amount of progress they make are largely the consequence of their own actions. These young people attribute success to factors that are largely under their own control. They realise that among the important influences are the sheer amount of hard work and practice applied to

Strengthening achievement motivation

Of course, having high achievement motivation does not guarantee success, and sometimes it results in a person having unrealistic expectations. But on the whole it is a definite asset. Other things being equal, someone with high achievement motivation will be likely to make more of their abilities than a person whose level of achievement motivation is lower.

That raises the question of whether it is possible to deliberately strengthen a person's achievement motivation. Although it is a relatively stable trait it is not immutable. So it ought to be possible to take steps that will increase it. A number of studies have explored the possibility of doing just that.

In one investigation, underachieving boys at an American summer camp were encouraged to set higher aspirations for themselves (Kolb, 1965). The results were very encouraging. There were definite

gains. Unfortunately, however, the advantages of simply encouraging higher aspirations were often short-lived in those participants who did not come from relatively affluent families, and these advantages tended to disappear after a year or so. It seems likely that with the poorer boys some follow-up support is necessary to ensure that the improvements become permanent.

Attempts to increase achievement motivation in people from non-Western cultures have also had some success. For example, David McClelland found that the introduction of a programme to train traders in rural India to think of themselves as potentially successful businessmen resulted in their being considerably more successful than comparable individuals who formed a control group (McClelland, 1978).

the task, acquired skills, concentration and willingness to persevere at a difficult task, having foresight and taking responsibility, and taking the trouble to make good plans. People like this implicitly acknowledge, along with Shakespeare's character Cassius in the play *Julius Caesar* (Act I, Scene II), that:

> *The fault, dear Brutus, is not in our stars,*
> *But in ourselves, that we are underlings.*

It is stretching a point to say that what we make of our lives is *entirely* in our hands. However, for many people, so far as learned accomplishments are concerned, the view expressed by Cassius is largely correct. In learning new skills, whether we succeed or fail at a task does greatly depend on our own efforts. People who fail to see this, and have (albeit through no fault of their own) a fatalistic perception of themselves as having no real control over their lives as learners, create big obstacles for themselves.

As we have seen, gaining a new skill or acquiring a body of knowledge can demand considerable effort and persistence. But, in the long run at least, getting involved in the learning process and persisting at it usually leads to mastery. Someone who realises that their eventual success or failure will depend on their own actions is much more likely to deal with learning problems effectively. Someone who fails to appreciate this, or believes that outcomes and rewards largely depend on outside influences and other people's efforts, will be much less likely to persist at attending to the learning task, and less inclined to engage in effective learning behaviours such as the ones that were described in Chapter 1. Consequently, at least in the long run, such a person will be far less successful at meeting his or her goals and enjoying a productive life than someone who does appreciate that everyone needs to face up to the responsibility for taking control over their lives.

Not surprisingly, young people's perceptions of locus of control are correlated with school achievement. There is a positive association between high achievement levels and the perception of control as being internal rather than external. Of course, the fact that the two are correlated does not prove that perceiving control to be internal actually *causes* high achievement. It is entirely possible that the positive correlation could be simply the outcome of other influences having a similar effect on achievement and locus of control. But, as we shall see, there have been some studies in which inducing children to change their perceptions of locus of control has had other positive effects. This finding suggests that locus of control is a genuinely influential factor.

Locus of control: the effects of making changes. In one study, teachers introduced a number of procedures that had the effect of giving the young children in their classrooms a greater degree of responsibility for organising their own learning activities (Matheny & Edwards, 1974). The researchers, who were interested in knowing whether doing this had any positive effects on the children's learning, found that it definitely did. For instance, there were big improvements in the children's reading. The value of giving children more responsibility was further underlined by the finding that the improvements were largest in those classrooms where the teachers were most successful at putting the new procedures into practice.

There were similar improvements in another classroom experiment. In this study 6-year-old pupils were encouraged to decide for themselves when to undertake the various kinds of school work that they had to do (Wang & Stiles, 1976). The teachers made the decisions about the learning tasks that had to be attempted, but instead of telling the children exactly when to do particular items of work, they allowed the children to choose that for themselves.

One result of making this change was to give the children increased feelings of control, as was evident from interviewing the children. But,

Changing children's feelings about control

In yet another classroom investigation older children, aged between 12 and 14, were explicitly encouraged to think about locus of control (de Charms, 1976). These pupils were taught to make a distinction between people who the teacher termed *pawns* and others who were called *origins*. Pawns were described as individuals who are controlled largely by outside forces: origins were described by the teacher as people who regard their activities as being under their own control. Unlike pawns, origins take responsibility for their actions and achievements, their successes and their failures, and are essentially in charge of their own lives.

After learning about this distinction the students were encouraged to think of themselves as being origins rather than pawns. The findings of the study were very encouraging. Not only did the students' *perceptions* of themselves change for the better, but their achievements at school also improved.

more importantly, the alteration also affected their studying behaviour. For instance, the proportion of the children's assignments that were successfully completed increased considerably.

Like the differences between individuals in achievement motivation, differences in perceived locus of control are related to family background. Individual differences seem to be largely the outcome of differing experiences, rather than being inherited. Compared with children with an external locus of control, those young people who perceive control as being internal are more likely to report that their parents were affectionate, supportive, and protecting, and inclined to give approval and praise rather than criticism (Collier, 1994).

However, there have been a few discrepant research findings. For instance, especially in girls, it appears that having parents who are helpful but overprotective may encourage children to be too dependent. Although warmth and protectiveness are essential in early childhood, at a later stage parents may need to be a little more cool and detached at times in order to encourage independence and discourage their child from relying on them too much.

Are perceptions of control the real issue? Some researchers have expressed the view that a person's *perceptions* of locus of control are not the real issue. It is possible, for instance, that differences between people on this dimension merely reflect individuals' awareness of the true state of affairs. According to this view, some people genuinely do have less control over their lives than others, for a variety of reasons. If this is true, then simply manipulating someone's perceptions of locus of control, without influencing the real circumstances of their life, may have little or no effect.

There may be some truth in that criticism, but research studies have nevertheless demonstrated that improvements can result from changing someone's perception of control, even when care has been taken to alter nothing else. For example, in one experiment it was found that people who were engaged at a proof-reading task worked less efficiently when their working environment became very noisy. However, when they were told that it was possible for them to reduce the noise level, the participants' performance improved, even if they did nothing to actually reduce the amount of noise (Glass & Singer, 1972).

Improvements in performance at school may result from altered perceptions of locus of control even in situations where no deliberate effort has been made to manipulate locus of control. In one American study, high-school volunteers who were poor at reading were paid to tutor younger backward readers (Cloward, 1967). The younger children's reading did improve, but there was a more dramatic improvement in the young people who were the tutors. Over the period in which they took part in the study their own reading improved considerably: they made twice the progress of comparable students in a control condition. It is possible that a number of different factors contributed to that outcome. Nonetheless, having more direct control over one's reading activities and more involvement in decision-making was almost certainly among the causes of the improvement.

Negative motivational influences: 1. Learned helplessness

Learned helplessness is a negative motivational influence that is related to the feeling of being controlled by external influences. As we have seen, the perception of having internal locus of control arises in part from experiencing situations in which a person's actions have predictable consequences. People differ in the extent to which their experiences have taught them to feel that they can exert control over their own lives.

Experiences of having control begin in infancy, as the psychologist Martin Seligman (1975, p.139) reported after observing his infant son;

> He sucks, the world responds with warm milk. He pats the breast, his mother tenderly squeezes him back. He takes a break and coos, his mother coos back... Each step he takes is synchronised with a response from the world.

During infancy, by making it evident that the baby has some power to make things happen, such experiences encourage a dawning awareness of having some control over aspects of one's life. The majority of children discover that their own actions are influential in a widening range of circumstances. Increasing ability to control things is an important aspect of becoming more independent, and as children get older they become more able to take responsibility for their actions and better equipped to take charge of their lives. But things can go wrong. Sometimes children grow up without feeling they have adequate control over the events that matter to them.

Mother breastfeeding. Photograph courtesy TRIP, photographer B. Turner

Martin Seligman, who was the first psychologist to use the term "learned helplessness", had noticed that when animals are kept in conditions that prevent them learning to connect their own actions with predictable consequences (by depriving them of situations in which effective behaviour reliably brings rewards), the animals tend to become withdrawn, unresponsive, and passive. Depriving them of any effective control over what happened to them seems to make it impossible for them to learn and function in a normal manner. Seligman thought that similar causes might contribute to some human learners becoming passive, isolated, indecisive, or depressed.

In practice, learned helplessness in children and adults is a matter of degree. Neither its causes nor its consequences are as straightforward

---

Learned helplessness in children: Possible causes

There are two particular kinds of circumstances that might bring about the state of affairs in which young people perceive themselves as being unable to take control of their lives:

- In the first, there is a lack of reliable and consistent reactions to the child's actions, perhaps because of neglect, or perhaps because a parent's behaviour towards the child is inconsistent and only arbitrarily related to that of the child. A consequence is that the child never learns to connect appropriate behaviours with rewards, and fails to learn that his or her own actions have predictable consequences.

- In the second scenario, parents who are over-indulgent and over-protective constantly flood the child with attention and rewards that take little account of the child's own behaviour. So, once again, despite all the attention he or she is given, the child fails to learn connections between his or her own actions and the events that follow them. In these circumstances, too, the child is unable to gain control because, once again, there is no clear relationship between actions and their consequences.

as in other animals. All the same, people who repeatedly experience failures and events that are outside their control often do develop an expectation, which may not be entirely unrealistic, that they are powerless and cannot influence the important events in their lives. Not surprisingly, these people may become apathetic and fatalistic, and they are liable to suffer from low self-esteem and depression.

Negative motivational influences: 2. Fear of failure

Fear of failure is another negative motivational influence. At first glance it would appear that the higher the level of someone's motivation, the better the consequences for learning. After all, the prospect of a huge reward is more attractive than a smaller one. But for various reasons the relationship between motivation and performance is not always quite as simple as that. Only up to a point is it true to say that the greater the incentive the harder we try. That is partly because when there is too much at stake people may become tense and nervous, with negative consequences. It is not that we do not want to do well, but we can become too anxious about the possibility of failing, sometimes with disastrous effects on our achievements.

In some circumstances, fear of failing can be a major disincentive to learning. In order to understand how that can happen, try to imagine that you are one of the slow learners in a school classroom, and your teacher sets you a new arithmetic problem. You have been slipping back recently, so compared with most of your classmates your knowledge and skills are weak. Consequently, however hard you try there is a good chance that you will fail. But nobody likes to fail, and it is more than likely that you will have learned to regard the experiences of failing as unpleasant if not humiliating. Therefore, from your perspective, it is important to avoid being in the situation of failing once again to achieve something you have tried to do.

But how do you avoid it? One way is by simply not trying. Doing that will not make you succeed at the task, but it will at least put off the humiliating consequences of failing to achieve something you have made an effort to do. From the outside, ceasing to try seems a wasteful and harmful way of dealing with learning problems. But young people who do not know any other way of avoiding shameful failures and protecting their all-important self-esteem will see things differently. They may be willing to pay that price.

Fear of failure stops many people making the best of their capabilities. Sadly, it is not at all uncommon. In a perfect world fear of failure would not exist at all, and the knowledge of having failed at a learning task would be seen as no more than helpful feedback, providing students and other learners with the useful information that mastery has not yet been achieved and more work still needs to be done. But for better or worse most people take failure more personally than that. Their self-esteem suffers. It takes an unusually self-confident individual to see that failing is just an indication of the level of performance achieved at one particular moment, rather than a sign that one has somehow failed as a person.

Fear of failure is not restricted to young people who usually do badly at school. From time to time most of us are afflicted by it. I can certainly think of times when worries about failing have held me back: this has certainly happened to me! Sadly, however, those learners who are most likely to be severely affected by fear of failure are the very people who have most to suffer from its consequences. Equally unfortunately, fear of failure is linked with individuals' perceptions of locus of control, with the two influences working together in a kind of vicious cycle. For someone who is always failing, it is some comfort to believe that success and failure depend on forces outside one's control. But as we have seen, holding that belief results in people making even less effort to make progress. And that, in turn, creates further failures.

The effects of an occasional failure are usually not disastrous: from time to time we all do badly. But for a child at school who encounters failure after failure the consequences may be dire. This is demonstrated by the findings of an experiment that was conducted to examine the outcome of experiencing repeated failures (Covington & Omelich, 1981). In this study it was discovered that participants who repeatedly failed to do well at tasks (which had been deliberately designed by the experimenters to make this inevitable) lowered their estimates of their own ability. They also became less happy, less confident of success in the future, and more likely to experience feelings of shame. As their failures mounted they became increasingly distressed and they experienced sentiments of hopelessness. Their perceived locus of control began to change. To try to maintain their self-esteem, they increasingly attributed their failures to external factors outside their influence. They also became increasingly inactive, and gave signs of feeling helpless.

It is important to remember that all these unhappy consequences of failing were produced in an artificial experiment, conducted over a period of just a few weeks, with participants who were college students and whose previous learning experiences had been at least reasonably positive. If the negative outcomes of failing that these individuals experienced as a result of participating in the study can be produced so easily and so quickly in basically self-confident young people, it is not hard to imagine what happens in real life to children who go on experiencing regular and frequent school failures over periods of years. For a child who has a long history of failing and every reason to lack self-confidence, and is anxious to avoid repeated experiences of failing, being passive and making little or no effort to learn may seem to be the best way to deal with an almost impossible situation. In circumstances like these, young people can feel themselves locked into a situation in which they just cannot succeed.

Of course, successful individuals are able to see their failures in a different light, as useful indicators of the need to keep on trying. But this is only because their experiences have taught them that persistence usually brings rewards. Some young people have rarely if ever had the opportunity to discover this. For these less fortunate individuals fear of failure causes difficulties that are not at all easy to eradicate.

In a young person who has already become accustomed to failing, the chances are that the negative self-perceptions associated with failure can only gradually be eliminated. Patient and supportive teaching will be necessary.

Negative motivational influences: 3. Fear of success

It is not at all hard to see how fear of failure can hold learners back, but the idea that students can be impeded by fear of *succeeding* may appear quite absurd. How can that be? What is remotely bothersome about doing too well? As it happens, there are a number of ways in which performing very well, or the prospect of it, can create problems that impede learning.

The suspicion that succeeding can create real difficulties was first raised when researchers studying achievement motivation discovered

---

Taking steps to reduce fear of failure

Successful attempts to reduce the problem need to contain three elements:

- First, it is important for teachers to make sure that the individuals are able to succeed most of the time at the learning tasks they do undertake.
- Second, it is equally necessary to help produce a state of affairs in which, when young people fail to reach their goals at the first attempt, they stop seeing this kind of failure in a totally negative light, as an unpleasant event that threatens their self-esteem and demonstrates their incapability of ever doing well.
- Third, young people need to start thinking of occasional failures as useful indicators. They can provide useful information, by telling us when we are going wrong, and they can help to increase a learner's determination to succeed.

---

that some of the findings that had been obtained from studies involving males did not apply to girls and young women. The basic problem is that succeeding can have negative consequences as well as positive ones. In women especially, people who are highly successful and want to do well may also fear some of the consequences of success.

It is possible that fear of success is present in many highly capable women, and also in a substantial number of men. It has been suggested that although these individuals definitely want to succeed, their anxieties about the consequences of doing so can make them hold back or try less hard than they would otherwise do. The women may believe that doing *too* well, especially in areas of expertise that are regarded as largely male preserves, may lead to social disapproval, or to the perception of themselves (by others) as being less feminine. Some women may even form an association in their minds (perhaps without being fully aware of it) between a lack of traditional femininity and social rejection.

But does all this actually happen? In the original investigation of the fear of success phenomenon by Matina Horner, men and women were asked to give their reactions to a hypothetical situation in which a person gets the highest marks in a class of medical students (Collier, 1994). Women were found to be much more likely than men to report negative concerns, such as the possibility of social rejection and related worries.

Subsequent studies have confirmed that the prospect of success really can produce genuine fears and concerns. What is more, the problems are not confined to women. They are probably more common in

"Some people conquer their fear of success, or never experience it at all." Photograph of Margaret Thatcher courtesy TRIP, photographer G. Grieves

females than in males, although the findings of a few studies have identified more fear of success in males than in females. The circumstances that are most likely lead to fear of success depend on the values and conventions that a society holds. When these alter, there are likely to be alterations in the situations that elicit anxieties about the consequences of success.

So long as sexual discrimination continues to exist, women's fears of rejection will be justified, particularly in occupations dominated by males. But fear of failure can also result from entirely different causes. For instance, there are circumstances in which success brings higher expectations and more responsibilities, and a genuinely increasing likelihood of failure. It can be difficult to deal with the pressures that arise, and the desire to avoid them has led some young people to tragically self-destructive acts.

Self-efficacy

Albert Bandura (1986) has introduced the term "self-efficacy" to refer to a person's broad belief in being able to have control over influential lifetime events. An individual's feelings of self-efficacy are related to a person's judgements of their own capabilities, as well as self-esteem, and also the motivational influences we have already introduced, including achievement motivation, perceived locus of control, fear of failure or success, and learned helplessness. Two people may have similar abilities but differ considerably in what they feel capable of achieving. Individual's beliefs about their own abilities are in some respects as crucial as the objective levels of those abilities. At all levels of ability, those individuals whose self-efficacy beliefs are high tend to be more successful at solving problems and more likely to persevere at effortful activities than others.

Perceptions of self-efficacy help to determine how a person responds to a new challenge. A high sense of self-efficacy is associated with various positive self-perceptions. It inclines a young person to be ambitious and adventurous, and eager to tackle new problems and demanding tasks. People who believe in their own powers tend to persist in spite of experiences of rejection or failure: in many spheres of life, fortune favours those who can keep going until they finally succeed. Conversely, low self-efficacy will make a person avoid challenges and disregard opportunities to master new capabilities. The belief that one is incapable of various choices can be a powerful negative influence. For instance, some young smokers attribute their failure to give up their habit to an inability to refuse their peers' offers of cigarettes (Durkin, 1995).

Self-efficacy levels are influenced by previous learning experiences, and also by family background variables. For example, in one study it was found that the children of depressed mothers saw themselves as being ineffective at helping other children deal with emotional problems (Garber, Braafledt, & Zeman, 1991).

Motivation: Conclusions

By now it is clear that in speaking of motivation one is not referring to one single influence on learning. Rather, it is a whole range of influences that can have various kinds of effects, depending on the circumstances. The relationships between motivation and learning are not always straightforward: a reward that provides an effective incentive for one kind of person in one set of circumstances may be less effective in different circumstances. For instance, as we have seen, although the praise and encouragement of adults is often helpful for children, particularly with new and unfamiliar activities, it can have negative effects when introduced in conjunction with activities that are intrinsically motivating.

As children get older, their interests and values alter and some of their needs wax or wane. Particular incentives become more or less effective. For a young child the attention of an adult is often a powerful reward, especially in a school classroom where adults are in short supply. But with increasing age most children attach more and more importance to the approval of their peers, and they may be decreasingly concerned about gaining adult attention.

Many different factors can affect the incentive value of a particular motivational influence. These include the individual's personality, age, and developmental stage, and various aspects of learning situations such as their perceived familiarity and difficulty. The aspects of motivation that we have examined in this chapter are some of the most important ones. These include achievement motivation, perceived locus of control, learned helplessness, fear of failure, fear of success, and the distinction between extrinsic and intrinsic incentives.

Photograph courtesy TRIP, photographer A. Cowin

Good learning and study habits

Being well motivated helps a person to gain abilities partly because it makes it easier to concentrate on the kinds of learning and practising tasks from which our capabilities are built: it gives someone a reason for learning. Another positive influence that helps a person to concentrate on learning activities is the establishment of a regular habit of learning or studying. Good working habits, once acquired, make it easier for people to get on with productive activities. In the absence of firm habits it is all too easy to waste time by not concentrating on the task at hand, and daydreaming, or thinking about other things, or wishing oneself elsewhere.

The benefits for learners of having formed good working habits was demonstrated in some American research. In a series of studies, early teenagers who were doing their regular everyday activities were briefly stopped at random times and asked to say what they were doing and how they felt about doing it (Csikszentmihalyi & Csikszentmihalyi, 1993). In particular, these young people had to say whether or not they were giving all their attention to the activity, and if they were enjoying whatever it was they were engaged in. The researchers discovered that the participants' responses strongly depended on the kind of activity they were involved in at the time. For example, if they were talking to their friends or listening to music they usually reported being alert and attentive and also enjoying what they were doing. If they were studying on their own, however, they often said they were feeling tired or finding it hard to concentrate, and indicated that they were not enjoying the study activity at all.

However, as we have seen, in order to succeed at school it is necessary to study conscientiously. There is plenty of evidence that those students who do manage to keep their minds on the study activities they are engaged in learn far more, and are much more successful, than students who cannot concentrate on studying. This was certainly true of the students in the present study. Amongst them, those individuals who reported not finding it too difficult to study on their own, and who said that they could concentrate when studying, were making substantially better progress than the other participants.

Here it is clear that there is an important question that needs answering: what is different about those teenagers who do find it possible to sustain their concentration on study activities, and are reasonably happy about studying, compared with those teenagers who report strongly disliking studying, and find it hard to maintain their attention to study tasks? To answer this, the researcher asked the students to provide various items of information about themselves, including information about their family backgrounds. He found that the home lives of virtually all those teenagers who experienced studying activities as positive had two characteristics:

- Predictably, their home environments encouraged learning and education, and provided stimulating environments.
- Less predictably, the homes were also ones in which substantial degrees of support and structure were evident.

The important point is that in the absence of support and structure, even the most stimulating family backgrounds did not guarantee that children would experience study and work activities in a positive light.

What precisely do we mean by a structured and supportive home background? This can be illustrated by contrasting the families in which these qualities were present with ones in which they were absent. First, the structured home background:

- Essentially, each member of the family contributed, shared jobs, had definite routines, gave assistance to others, had various responsibilities and knew what these were, and could always count on the support of other family members when it was needed.
- These families gave young people the security to get on with their lives, knowing what was expected of them and what they could count on, and confident that help was available when it was needed.
- Young people brought up in these home backgrounds learned to get on with whatever they were expected to do. They acquired the kinds of habits that make it easier for a person to get jobs done, including ones that involve learning and studying.

In an unstructured home background, on the other hand, even if it was a highly stimulating one, help and support could not be counted on. Typically:

- Home life was less predictable, and rules were arbitrary or unclear, or not reliably applied.
- In such a family a child who was asked to help with a routine chore might waste a lot of energy arguing about whose turn it

was to help and feeling resentful about the situation, or squabbling with other members of the family.

- A request by the same child for assistance by other members of the family would tend to produce similar arguments and grumbles, leading to further feelings of resentment and wasted emotional energy.
- Young people in these homes tended to waste a lot of time in activities that prevented them getting on with necessary tasks. These young people tended *not* to gain good working and studying habits.

Of course, most young people's home backgrounds are neither invariably supportive nor always unstructured: most are somewhere between these extremes. Moreover, the advantages that the more supportive families give a young person may only be temporary, and many individuals eventually learn to organise their own lives to a reasonable extent even when their families are somewhat chaotic.

All the same, young people whose structured and supportive family backgrounds encourage them to take on responsibilities, and to know they can rely on having plenty of support from parents or other members of the family, do have a clear advantage. They are helped to acquire the habit of getting on with whatever needs to be done, and persevering at the various study and learning activities that enable people to extend their abilities and gain new ones.

Summary

The learning that contributes to human abilities is affected by a number of broader influences. Attending is crucial. Differences between people in the extent to which they attend and in the manner in which they attend have important consequences. Attending is itself affected by acquired skills and habits.

Various kinds of motivation affect learning. External and internal forms of motivation are both necessary, but influence learning differently. Positive motivational influences include achievement motivation and internal locus of control, both of which can be strengthened by making appropriate interventions. Negative motivational influences include learned helplessness, fear of failure, and fear of success.

The acquisition of human abilities is also affected by various learning habits. Successful learners rely on good study habits, which can positively influence the effectiveness of an individual's efforts to learn.

Further reading

For a full account of the ways in which various kinds of motivational influences affect learning see G. Collier (1994), *Social origins of mental ability* (New York: Wiley). The importance of study habits for learning in young people is explained in M. Csikszentmihalyi, K. Rathunde & S. Whalen (1993), *Talented teenagers: The roots of success and failure* (New York: Cambridge University Press).

Towards more advanced abilities 5

T his chapter concentrates on how people gain the kinds of capabilities that are typically acquired in mid-childhood and later. As with the more basic capacities that a child acquires early in life, most of the accomplishments that are learned later involve a combination of knowledge and mental skills. Of course, the particular kinds of knowledge and skills that are gained can vary enormously from one area of expertise or knowledge to another. Also, there may be correspondingly large differences in the actual kinds of learning that are needed in order for a person to make progress. Consequently, for example, the steps by which someone becomes an expert mathematician are very different from those that lead to high levels of competence at sports, or music, or chess, or foreign languages. However, this chapter gives more emphasis to what various capabilities share in common than to their unique aspects.

Recall the three main principles of human learning that were described in Chapter 1. These were:

1. Learning takes place as the result of active mental processing.
2. Human abilities are gained and extended as a result of learning that involves perceiving meaningful connections between new information and the learner's existing knowledge.
3. Repetition aids learning.

These three principles are just as applicable to the kinds of learning that enable a person to gain relatively advanced skills and knowledge as they are to the simple and basic abilities that were discussed in previous chapters. In the following sections we shall see how they operate in practice. Keep in mind that in everyday learning, more often than not at least two of the three principles operate at the same time, and sometimes all three work together. Consider, for instance, a situation in which a mature student is reading some fairly difficult new material. She adopts a strategy in which she rephrases the content in her own words and then rehearses the new version. Here we can see that the student is (1) taking an active role by mentally transforming the information and (2) connecting the new information to her existing knowledge, and then, (3) by rehearsing, adopting the principle of repetition.

Applying learning principles: 1 & 2. Active mental processing and forming meaningful connections

As children get older they become increasingly adept at selecting learning methods that are appropriate to the particular school tasks that confront them. Compared with a younger child, the more sophisticated individual has made progress in "learning how to learn". As a result, the mature person may frequently be able to choose a learning strategy or technique that is particularly effective. The older individual is likely to have more success than a young child at first assessing the demands of the learning task, and then taking sensible steps to ensure that new knowledge is gained or a new skill is mastered.

Even when using a learning aid that is available to young children, the older learner still has advantages. For example, when introducing a strategy such as rehearsing, the more mature individual will have a better understanding of (a) the amount of rehearsal that is likely to be necessary and also (b) the particular kind of rehearsing that is most appropriate.

Most older students make regular use of a variety of learning strategies, methods, and techniques, often without giving the matter much conscious thought. These provide the "tools of the trade" that aid the effective learner. For instance, in the course of a single morning spent studying, at various times a student may:

- organise and divide up information that has to be learned;
- look for familiar ideas in a passage describing something unfamiliar;
- underline important words and concepts;
- take notes;
- provide brief summaries of key contents;
- make up a rhyme or sentence to connect unconnected facts; and perhaps even
- form a visual image to make something easier to recall.

Self-testing (mentioned in Chapter 1) is yet another kind of activity that mature learners rely on. This can have two useful results: it helps people to monitor their progress and it also performs a kind of repetition or practice function.

Using specific memory aids

From time to time many students make use of what are call "first-letter mnemonics". These can help a person to learn by making information easier to remember. (The word *mnemonic* simply means a memory aid.) For example, the sentence "*Richard of York Gave Battle In Vain*" provides an easy way of remembering the colours in the rainbow: Red, Yellow, Green, Blue, Indigo, Violet. Here it is clear that the (relatively) meaningful sentence aids memory by forming a method for combining several items of information that would otherwise be separate. Rhymes can provide a similar function, forming a thread linking a number of items, as in "*i before e except after c*", or "*Thirty days hath September...*".

There are also a number of helpful learning techniques that involve students forming visual images of items that need to be remembered. These techniques provide further demonstrations of the advantages of taking an active approach to learning. However, the benefits are usually somewhat restricted, the main use of these memory aids being to help people learn lists of separate items.

Most imagery-based learning techniques are fairly similar to one another. Typically, they involve forming a concrete visual image of one or more items, and then making a connection between that image and

another visual image. For example, with one method for helping learners to retain lists of unrelated words the student starts by forming an image in which objects representing the first two words are combined with each other. So, in order to remember a list starting with *bottle, envelope, table, window*, a student might begin by forming a visual image of a bottle wrapped by an envelope. Next, a clear image is made of an envelope resting on a table, followed by an image of a table in front of a window. This system works well, and it provides a way to remember longs list of words, such as shopping lists. As soon as the first word is recalled the corresponding visual image can be made to appear. Because that image contains the object depicting the second word, the latter can easily be recalled. The image of that word in turn elicits the third word, and by following the same procedure it is eventually possible to recall the whole list. A limitation of this technique is that it is fairly time-consuming. This is because two images have to be made for each word, and it takes most people at least several seconds to form a clear visual image.

One technique that cuts down on the number of images that have to be made involves starting by learning this simple rhyme:

One is a bun	Six are sticks
Two is a shoe	Seven is heaven
Three is a tree	Eight is a gate
Four is a door	Nine is wine
Five is a hive	Ten is a hen

It takes a few minutes to learn the rhyme, but once that has been done it can be used again and again. To use this method, the learner first has to form a clear visual image of each of the nouns in the rhyme: bun, shoe, tree, and so on. Then, when presented with a list of words that need to be remembered, all that is necessary is to form a visual image of the first item connected with a bun, the second item with a shoe, the third with a tree, and so forth. When the items need to be recalled, the person starts reciting the rhyme silently from the beginning, and re-activates the image of the bun. That elicits the connected image, enabling the individual to remember the corresponding word. And as the rhyme proceeds, each successive word from the list can be retrieved.

Using the keyword method to learn foreign-language words

Procedures similar to the ones just described have proved effective in helping students to learn new words in a foreign language. One useful technique is known as the *keyword method*. This provides an effective way of forming connections between foreign language words and their English equivalents.

The keyword system works because it changes the nature of the learning task from one that people find difficult — making a connection between two completely unrelated words — to one that people find easier, namely forming connections based on similar sounds and visual images. Ostensibly, the learning has been made more complicated,

---

Using the keyword method

Here is how the keyword method works. Imagine that a student needs to retain the information that the Russian word *zvonok* means *bell* in English.

1. The first step is to select a keyword. This is simply an English word that has a similar sound to the foreign word. For instance, as the Russian word *zvonok* sounds like "zvan-oak" an effective keyword would be the noun *oak*.
2. Once provided with an appropriate keyword, the student learns the connection between it and the Russian word. Because of their similarity in sound, this is easy to do.
3. Making that connection provides one of two links that the learner forms. The second link to be made is between the keyword and the English word that means the same as the foreign word. In the present example the link has to be formed between *oak* and *bell*. This second link is achieved via a visual image. What the learner actually does in this instance is to form a clear visual image in which the two objects, *oak* and *bell* are combined.

---

because the task has been changed from one that involves learning just one connection to one in which two separate links have to be retained. However, this is compensated for by the fact that it is no longer necessary to retain an arbitrary connection involving unrelated items.

There have been a number of evaluations of the effectiveness of the keyword method in practice, and it has been found to work well. For example, in one study students learned a total of 120 Russian words over a three-day period. At the end, it was found that participants who were shown how to use the keyword method could recall 72% of the words, whereas students who had learned the words using a conventional rote technique recalled only 46% of the words. When a follow-up test was administered six weeks later, those students who had used the keyword method could remember 50% more words than the other learners (Atkinson, 1975).

The keyword technique also yielded similar improvements in a much longer-term study. This extended over a nine-week period. During that time university students enrolled in a Russian language course tried to learn a total of about 700 words (Raugh & Atkinson, 1975). Once again the keyword method was found to be effective. It is also significant that when students were given the choice of using the method or not using it, they did choose it, and they did so increasingly as the nine-week period progressed.

These findings confirm that the success of the method is not simply an outcome of its novelty. On the contrary, students continue to find the keyword technique worthwhile long after its novelty has worn off.

Note-taking

Taking notes is a study technique that is widely used by students. It can be used in conjunction with taught classes and lectures, and also in connection with reading from books. There is not really a right or wrong way of taking notes, although for obvious reasons it is important to the note-taker to ensure that the most crucial material is reproduced.

- Sometimes it is desirable to have notes that are as full and detailed as possible, but on other occasions all that is necessary is to write down a few key words that will serve as a memory-aid.
- In some instances it is necessary to record as literally as possible the content of a book, article, or lecture. At other times it is better to transform the material into one's own words. Having to do that is likely to make information more memorable because it maximises the active mental processing involved.

Depending on the particular kinds of note-taking activities involved, taking notes is likely to be useful for the following reasons.

1. First, and most obviously, a convenient record is provided of needed information.
2. Also, the actual activity of taking notes aids learning. That is partly because it helps to ensure that the learner is being mentally active and attending carefully. The extent to which note-taking will encourage mental activity will depend on the particular nature of the note-taking activities involved. Just writing down important words will at least serve the function of keeping the learner alert, even if it achieves nothing more than that. Rephrasing the information into the learner's own words will ensure that a more substantial amount of mental processing will occur.
3. Particularly when note-takers make a genuine effort to translate the content into their own words, notes provide the learner with a version that is especially helpful because it definitely makes sense to the person concerned.

Applying learning principles: 3. Practice and training

Many of the capabilities that we value most are only gained as a result of a person making considerable efforts over substantial periods of time. As was explained in Chapter 1, repetition and rehearsal are essential ingredients of learning. These activities can take various forms. They range from the kinds of practising activities that lead to mastery of a musical instrument or a performing skill such as dancing, to the exercises and problem-solving activities that build a person's competence in science and mathematics.

Photograph courtesy TRIP, photographer G. Kufner

The activity of practising tends to be taken for granted. It can be arduous and sometimes boring. It is rarely glamorous or exciting. Nevertheless, in many areas of expertise practising is absolutely vital for success. It is sometimes suggested that there are certain gifted people who can get ahead in a skill area without having to practise, but that is simply a myth. In music, for instance, the number of hours spent practising an instrument turns out to be the best single predictor of a person's level of competence.

Successful practising

Practising is not always fun. Like it or not, the kinds of practising that some people find boring may be just as necessary as those practising activities that are more interesting. In music, for instance, research has established that doing formal exercises such as scales, which even successful learners often do not enjoy, is essential for making good progress. In one investigation it was discovered that young players who were doing especially well at their instrument not only spent more time practising than less successful young people, but devoted a greater proportion of their practice time to scales and technical exercises (Sloboda, Davidson, Howe, & Moore, 1996).

Because practising is not always interesting, even enthusiastic learners often need support and guid-ance. Inexperienced musicians tend to play through whole pieces without stopping, but in order to make good progress it is necessary to divide a passage into parts and repeatedly practise those elements that are causing difficulty. The majority of successful young musicians are individuals who have been helped to practise by their parents. There are very few young learners who do not find it hard to motivate themselves to practise at times, and adult encouragement is vital. Even the most able musicians often admit that had it not been for their parents' support and encouragement during childhood they would never have managed to keep persevering at essential practice activities, especially the more formal activities that are based on scales and technical exercises (Sloboda & Howe, 1991).

This does not mean that practising on its own can produce high levels of mastery, or that the sheer amount of time spent practising is all-important. Other important factors include the appropriateness of the particular practising activities in which the learner engages. A good teacher can make a large difference here. Another important influence is the learner's degree of commitment. Learners who practise enthusiastically and concentrate on the task make far more progress than people who simply go through the motions.

As was mentioned in Chapter 1, it can take many years of training and practice to reach high levels of mastery. Becoming an international chess player usually takes at least 10 years of sustained preparation. Similar periods of concentrated training are needed in order to reach the highest levels of mastery in other fields, such as science, mathematics, various sports, and composing. Even with a genius like Mozart, who is known to have composed music in early childhood, it was not until he had been working hard at music for 10 years or so that he became capable of those compositions that we regard as being his major works.

The idea of expertise

In the past, psychologists generated numerous theories of learning and did large numbers of experiments on learning, more often in rats and other animals than in humans. The hope was that all this research activity would lead to a full understanding of the basic processes underlying learning. It was thought that it would then be possible to apply this theoretical knowledge to the real world, basing educational and instructional procedures on the understanding of learning that the research had generated. Sadly, however, that goal proved elusive, for various reasons:

- One problem was that the varieties of learning that had been studied in non-human species such as rats proved to have little relevance for the kinds of human learning that make it possible for people to gain knowledge and skills.
- Conversely, there are important kinds of learning that are possible only for humans. Because they have the huge advantage of possessing a language, humans have access to learning processes and mechanisms that are not available to other animals. As we saw in Chapter 2, having language greatly magnifies and extends the power to gain new abilities.
- In particular, human learners, unlike animals, can make use of their capacity to communicate ideas to other people. Language also makes it possible for people to communicate *to themselves*, as is done in human thinking and reasoning.
- Also, because we have language, which enables people to store information in symbolic form, we can retain events in memory and remember events in the past. That, in turn, makes planning future actions possible and enables the learner to draw on knowledge gained on a previous occasion.

Apart from the disappointingly limited practical applicability of animal-based research into learning, another problem emerged. This was that many of the most important questions about how people gain competence cannot be answered simply on the basis of a knowledge of learning processes as such. This is apparent if we consider a typical practical question related to the acquisition of a capability, such as, "How can we help young people to become expert musicians?" As soon as we start to think seriously about what we would need to know in order to do this, it becomes clear that knowledge about learning processes provides just one of a number of kinds of information that are needed. Other kinds of information are just as crucial. For instance: what exactly are the skills that a good musician possesses? How is a competent performer different from a beginner? What stages of competence does a beginner need to pass through in order to gain the capabilities of an expert? What is the best route to becoming an expert?

The fact that we have to be able to answer questions like these ones in order to be able to help young learners demonstrates that we require more than just a knowledge of learning processes as such. In order to teach effectively we also have to know about the nature of the skill being learned and about the most effective routes for making progress. This is rather like observing that in order to walk to the South Pole it is not enough to be a good walker. Walking is involved, certainly, but other kinds of expertise and knowledge are just as crucial.

Awareness of these complications has led to researchers who are interested in helping people learn new skills and capabilities to stress that more is involved than learning processes. Psychologists have begun to pay attention to the other kinds of knowledge necessary for helping people to gain new capabilities.

Research on expertise is an expanding area of activity by psychologists and educators. It aims to understand the detailed nature of the various skills and capabilities that are possessed by an expert in a particular field or domain of ability. This knowledge makes it possible to help others to become experts.

Pioneering research into expertise concentrated on the game of chess. Here it is relatively easy to rate someone's degree of expertise and to identify the differences between a good player and a novice. When shown a chess position and asked to select the best next move, good players consistently choose moves that are more appropriate. Players can be encouraged to think aloud as they select their move.

Photograph
courtesy TRIP,
photographer
M. Peters

Using the information that this yields, it is then possible to examine the nature of the differences in the mental operations introduced by experts and novices. Similar kinds of analysis are possible with other kinds of expertise.

Gaining exceptional abilities

The highest levels of ability and the people who achieve them are especially interesting. The greatest human achievements do not only benefit their creators but may also have large influences on other people. Millions of people have enjoyed the masterpieces of creative geniuses like Mozart and Shakespeare, and numerous lives have been profoundly affected by the achievements of great scientists such as Newton and Darwin.

In this section we examine some of the causes that contribute to individuals becoming exceptionally skilled or exceptionally knowledgeable. There is a tendency to think that, because exceptional achievements can be so greatly superior to anything that seems to be within the capabilities of ordinary people, the origins of those achievements must also be very different. On the whole this is untrue, however. We can certainly learn more about outstanding capabilities by looking at what they have in common with more mundane capacities than by becoming too awed by what is special and different about the most impressive human abilities.

Motivation and high achievements

When people are asked what is special about those individuals who have the most impressive abilities of all, they produce words like "intelligent", "creative", "knowledgeable", and "fluent". A component of very high levels of ability that is less often mentioned but just as important is strong *motivation*.

As we saw in Chapter 4, motivation is a major influence on learning. It has a variety of effects on the abilities people gain. Almost without exception, those men and women who become capable of high levels of achievement in a particular field of expertise are strongly motivated to do so. Take, for instance, those rare individuals whom we acknowledge for achievements that are especially exceptional and important by calling "geniuses". In most respects geniuses are very different from one another. But one attribute is shared by virtually all geniuses: they are very strongly motivated. The powerful motivation that is typical of individuals who gain exceptional abilities has a number of aspects:

1. People who become exceptionally able have a very strong sense of direction. They know what they want to do.
2. Such individuals tend to be strongly focused on particular goals and aspirations.
3. As a result, they resist distractions and avoid getting side-tracked. They are good at concentrating their energies in a particular direction.
4. These people usually work very hard at acquiring the capabilities they need. Exceptionally able people may appear to work fluently and effortlessly, but that is only possible because of all the effort that has already gone into mastering the skills on which their achievements depend.

Immense determination is a characteristic feature of the highest achievers. They have a capacity to concentrate exclusively — and keep on concentrating — on one particular task or problem. For example:

- In the case of Mozart, a number of his contemporaries remarked on the capacity he had to give all his attention to whatever he was doing. Even when he was a young child it was noticed that "whatever he was set to learn he gave himself to so completely that he put aside everything else". When working on music, he appeared completely unaware of everything else. As one observer recalled, "As soon has he began to give himself to music, all his senses were as good as dead to other occupations" (Schenk, 1960, p.29).
- Newton, asked how he discovered the law of universal gravi-

---

Motivation and high achievement: 1. The case of Isaac Newton

No-one was more dogged or determined than Isaac Newton, the great seventeenth-century scientist. He worked as hard as anyone possibly could, to the extent that one of his contemporaries remarked that if it had not been for the relief gained by having to switch to the manual tasks involved in constructing his experiments, he would have "killed himself with study". Whenever Newton was learning something new, he kept at the task with immense determination, refusing to be defeated. When learning from a book, if he came to something he could not understand he went back to the beginning and started all over again. As someone who knew Newton when he was teaching himself mathematics from Descartes's *Geometry* reported (John Conduit, quoted in Westfall, 1980, p. 111), finding himself stuck and unable to understand after two or three pages, Newton

…began again & got 3 or 4 pages farther till he came to another difficult place, then he began again & advanced farther and continued doing till he had made himself Master of the whole without having the least light or instruction from any body.

tation, replied, "By thinking upon it continuously" (Westfall, 1980, p.110).

- Albert Einstein was similarly able to direct ferocious and sustained concentration on problems: he refused to be diverted or distracted. Einstein considered that his achievements were rooted in his passionate curiosity rather than in any special gift.
- Charles Darwin, who insisted that he was not particularly quick or clever, said that the keys to his own success lay in curiosity, determination, and sheer hard work, combined with "the patience to reflect or ponder for any number of years over any unexplained problem" (Darwin, 1958, p.140).

These qualities can make a person seem eccentric, and difficult to live with. There are stories of Newton neglecting to eat and forgetting to sleep at times when he was absorbed with a problem. Einstein too neglected everyday matters. He was known to absent-mindedly write equations all over an expensive tablecloth, or kneel on the floor and scribble diagrams on a scrap of paper on a chair if no table happened to be available.

Motivation and high achievement: 2. Sir Richard Burton

It would be wrong to suggest that strong motivation is *the* dominant component of genius, but it clearly does play a major role among the causes of high achievements. Motivation can help to explain some unusual patterns of abilities. Consider, for example, the case of Sir Richard Burton (1821–1890).

Burton was a notable explorer. He led expeditions searching for the origins of the Nile and was among the first Britons to enter the forbidden holy city of Mecca. He was also a quite remarkable linguist, mastering around 30 foreign languages, and translating into English a substantial amount of Indian, Persian, Arabic, and Portuguese prose and poetry, including the 16-volume *Arabian Nights*. He also published many other books and made major contributions to archaeology, ethnology, anthropology, botany, zoology, and geology.

How can we account for one single person's gaining such a remarkable collection of capabilities? Diverse as these capacities were, most of them depended on Burton's exceptional command of languages. But how did that emerge? Motivational factors can supply some useful clues here. For instance:

1. Burton's childhood was spent largely abroad, and as an outgoing youngster he frequently encountered situations in which there were advantages to be gained from learning to communicate with other people who did not speak English.

So, right from the outset, learning new languages was a useful thing for him to do. And that quickly produced real rewards for Burton: it was not just the pointless school activity that it has appeared to be for too many children.

2. In consequence, by the time Burton became an adult the activity of learning new languages would been a familiar one. As well as having discovered for himself that it brought useful advantages, he would have gained the self-confidence that comes from the experience of having succeeded at it in the past. He would also have gained various kinds of knowledge and skill that apply to language learning in general.

Just as geniuses such as Darwin and Einstein insisted that they had no special gift or aptitude for learning, Burton believed that he had no special facility for language. Like them, he attributed his remarkable success to sheer hard work. There was nothing very unusual about the learning techniques he followed. But in common with the exceptional achievers we have already mentioned, Burton was immensely determined, dogged, and persistent. He struggled on until he reached his goals, however long it took and however much difficulty was involved.

For instance, when learning Hindustani he complained at spending 12 hours every day on what he called "a desperate struggle" to master the language (Brodie, 1971, p.54). But he kept going, all the same, long after the vast majority of people would have slowed down or given up entirely. Only someone with the immense determination and self-confidence that Burton's earlier learning experiences had given him could have succeeded in those circumstances.

High intelligence levels and high abilities

People who are high achievers at the areas of expertise that depend on knowledge and intellectual skills tend to be highly intelligent. They typically get high intelligence test scores (IQs). That is hardly surprising, as the skills assessed in intelligence tests are often similar to the skills on which expertise depends.

However, the relationship between high abilities and high intelligence test scores is only a loose one. Even with activities as cerebral as playing chess, the correlations between degree of expertise and IQ are low. Moreover, although having at least a fairly high intelligence level is necessary in various areas of achievement, those individuals whose IQs are exceptionally high usually do no better than people whose intelligence level is fairly high but not outstandingly so (Howe, 1990). For example, consider some of the findings of a large-scale study conducted in California by Lewis Terman. It was discovered that in a group of people who all had high IQs, a knowledge of their precise scores did not help to predict which individuals among them would eventually be the highest achievers. When the 150 men in the study who were most successful of all were compared with the 150 who were the least successful, there was found to be no difference between them in their average childhood IQ scores (Ceci, 1990).

It has also been suggested that, although it is true that people who gain high intelligence test scores tend to do well in their careers, this does not necessarily mean that they succeed *because of* their high IQs. This is a controversial matter, with some psychologists claiming that the qualities assessed in intelligence tests are vital for high achievements, while others argue that IQ scores predict achievement simply because they happen to be correlated with other influences such as education and social class. With some kinds of success in life, IQ appears to remain a good predictor even when these other important influences on achievement are held constant (Herrnstein & Murray, 1994). This suggests that the qualities assessed in an IQ test do play an important role. However, with other criteria of success the relationship between IQ level and achievement decreases to almost zero when other influences are held constant, indicating that the qualities that determine a person's IQ scores are less important (Ceci, 1990).

As was seen in Chapter 3, people with low IQ scores are sometimes capable of impressive mental skills. And even in the most favourable circumstances, IQ tests are far from being perfect instruments for making predictions about people's future success. The correlations that have been calculated as a way of quantifying relationships observed between test scores and various kinds of achievements account for no more than around 20% of the variability between people. Indeed, with certain groups of people IQ scores are not even adequate measures of the kinds of everyday intelligence that contribute to their success in life. For example, in an investigation of the abilities of a large sample of Chinese immigrants to the United States, it was discovered that their IQs were below average. Despite that, they were very successful at their work, with almost twice as many of them gaining professional status than was true of the American population in general (Flynn, 1991).

Innate gifts and talents

A widespread view is that in order to achieve the very highest levels of expertise a person has to possess certain inborn qualities in the form of innate gifts or innate talents. It is often thought, for example, that only someone with an appropriate innate talent can aspire to be, say, an outstanding musician or an exceptional artist or sportsperson.

Is that view really true? It certainly appears to be, and everyday common sense suggests that it is. Also, there undoubtedly exist immense differences between people in the progress they make in various skill areas. It is not uncommon, for example, to hear of families in which one child struggles for years with very little success to learn a musical instrument but a younger brother or sister takes to the instrument with apparent naturalness and seems to make more progress with less effort. This seems to confirm that some children are innately talented, while others are not. Also, there is strong evidence that some of the ways in which people differ genetically have influences that make it more or less likely that one individual will flourish in a particular field of expertise.

So people certainly are different from each other, in ways that seem to make their success at various kinds of skill more or less likely. But when people say that a child is innately talented, they are usually implying more than this. People rarely make it clear exactly what they mean by the word talent, but they believe that there is some special inherited quality that can be identified early in life which makes it possible to predict whether or not a particular child will be capable of reaching high levels of accomplishment in the talent area. In music, for example, most of the teachers who decide which children are to be given advance instruction believe that young people cannot thrive in music unless they possess an innate gift for music (Sloboda, Davidson, & Howe, 1994).

The fact that many teachers hold that view has important consequences for individual children. For example, a child who is believed not to be talented is unlikely to be offered the special training that is needed in order to succeed as a musician. So if it was found that the belief in the idea of innate talents in some children was not actually justified, it would be clear that some children would have been unfairly excluded from valuable opportunities to learn. If only to rule out the possibility that such unjustified — and unfair — discrimination against some children is occurring, it is important to try to establish whether it is true or untrue that innate talents actually exist.

Evidence for and against the talent account

There are various kinds of evidence that seem to confirm the talent account, according to which some children, but not others, possess special innate talents that:

- have genetic origins;
- can be identified in childhood, enabling trained people to identify that talent is present at an early stage;
- make it possible to predict which children are likely to excel;
- are only present in a minority of individuals; and
- are specific to particular fields of accomplishment.

First, there have been some reports suggesting that in some children abilities may emerge spontaneously and unusually early, in the absence of opportunities for training and practising. For example, according to one account a boy began speaking at 5 months of age and had a 50-word vocabulary a month later. Another child was described as speaking in sentences at 3 months and reading simple books by his first birthday. In addition, in biographical reports of the early lives of prominent musicians there are a number of anecdotes that appear to point to remarkable feats in early childhood. For example, Arthur Rubenstein claimed to have mastered the piano before he could speak.

However, the reliability of these accounts is questionable. In most cases they were provided by proud parents. In no instance were the very precocious language skills directly observed by a researcher. The reports of spontaneous early skills in musicians are usually based on autobiographical accounts. These are especially dubious in view of the fact that research has established that people can recall almost nothing of their first three years. In those individuals whose unusual musical skills in early childhood are well documented, such as Mozart, it is clear that the child had received considerable training by the time the precocious skills emerged. Mozart practised intensively from a very early age.

A second kind of evidence that appears to support the view that innate talents exist takes the form of accounts of a special capacity that appears to facilitate the acquisition of specific (musical) abilities, and is present in only a minority of individuals. Some young children have a capacity for "perfect" or "absolute" pitch perception. That makes it possible for them to sing specified pitches very accurately. Young musicians who possess perfect pitch have clear advantages over other children.

Once again, however, there are a number of complications. We cannot be sure that evidence of perfect pitch in certain children demonstrates the existence of innate talent. One problem is that although perfect pitch appears in early childhood, it is gained through learning and experience, rather than being innate. Another objection to the suggestion that perfect pitch provides proof of an innate talent is that although it gives a young instrumentalist certain advantages, the benefits are not unrestricted. It is significant that among professional musicians, those who do have absolute pitch are by no means always more successful than those who do not.

The third body of findings that are apparently consistent with the talent account comes from a large number of studies that have looked for evidence of biological involvement in special abilities. There is a substantial body of research pointing to relationships between abilities and various measures of brain structure and function. This evidence is certainly consistent with the view that innately determined biological differences between people make a contribution to the fact that people differ in their levels of expertise in various areas of achievement.

All the same, however, none of the findings points to influences that are anything like as direct and specific as innate talents are believed to be. And while high abilities correlate with brain measures, differences between people in the physical characteristics of their brains are in some cases the result rather than the cause of individual differences in learning and experience (Howe, Davidson, & Sloboda, 1998).

Contrasting with the evidence that appears to support the talent account, there are other research findings that seem to contradict it. First, opposing the aforementioned findings that seem to point to early signs of high abilities, there is a substantial body of evidence pointing to an absence of those early indications of special skills that would be consistent with the talent account. Firm evidence of early indicators of unusual expertise have been surprisingly absent. This is despite the fact that a number of studies have examined the early progress of individuals who have eventually reached exceptional levels of accomplishment in various spheres, in order to ascertain whether these individuals had shown early signs of being unusually promising. For instance, studies of tennis players, swimmers, musicians, artists, and mathematicians have reported very few early signs of unusual promise prior to the time at which parents began to encourage their child to excel (Howe, 1990).

There was a similar lack of early signs of future success in an investigation of outstanding American pianists in their mid-thirties who were on the brink of careers as concert pianists. As children, these individuals displayed few indications of future success, and when they did start to make unusually fast progress it appeared to be a result of having good opportunities and plenty of encouragement (Sosniak, 1985). Even when these young pianists had been having intensive training for six years or so, only in a minority would it have been possible to make confident predictions about their eventual outstanding success. Another investigation of children who had been given musical training found that those individuals who were eventually most successful were no more likely than those who were less successful to have displayed early indicators of possible future promise, such as moving to music, showing a liking for music or being especially attentive to it (Howe, Davidson, Moore, & Sloboda, 1995).

As we discovered in Chapter 2, it is true that children differ in the age at which they gain particular skills: for example it has been observed that babies in certain African tribes display capabilities such as walking, standing, and sitting about a month earlier than most children in other continents. However, it was subsequently discovered that the superior progress extended only to those particular skills that were specially trained by the parents (Super, 1976). In the traditional villages of the tribes concerned, the mothers strongly encourage early development of these abilities. Children who come from exactly the same tribes but have been brought up away from the traditional villages, and whose mothers do not conform to the traditional tribal practices, do not gain these abilities any earlier than children from other continents.

A second body of research findings that appear to contradict rather than support the talent account is provided by studies that have investigated the amount of time and training that is required in order to reach high levels of achievement. If innate talents play a vital role it would be expected that there would be some (talented) individuals who are able to make the same amount of progress as ordinary people with far less time and effort. However, that does not seem to happen. In music, for example, it takes at least 10 years of intensive training for even the greatest classical composers to produce those compositions that have gained a secure place in the repertoire. Chess players require comparable periods of study to reach the highest levels, as do experts in other areas including mathematics and various sports (Hayes, 1981).

A third and final group of findings that are inconsistent with the talent account has been produced by a number of studies in which adults who appear to be quite ordinary and without any signs of having special gifts or talents are given large amounts of training at special skills, typically ones that make heavy demands on memory. On a number of occasions it has been found that, following training, these people have reached levels of competence beyond what is generally believed to be possible. Uninformed observers of their feats have been seen to remark that the individual concerned must have possessed a special innate aptitude (Ericsson & Faivre, 1988).

Similarly, it is found that in certain cultures people regularly reach standards of performance that in another culture would be considered quite exceptional. This happens in relation to a variety of skills, ranging from swimming and canoeing to navigation over land or water

(Howe, 1990). The finding that levels of performance which appear to us to indicate special talents are in fact quite commonplace in certain other cultures seems to indicate that it is special experiences rather than innate talents that provide the key to high accomplishment.

If innate talents are not the cause of exceptional levels of accomplishment at particular abilities, what is the real cause? It is possible that the influences that lead to some individuals becoming exceptionally skilled are not so very different from the factors that lead to differences between people within normal levels of achievement. These include a number of causes that have already been mentioned, such as:

- Previously gained knowledge and skills.
- Attentiveness and concentration.
- Interests and preferences.
- Motivation and competitiveness.
- Self-confidence.
- Other temperament and personality variables.
- Enthusiasm and energy.

Prodigies

The word prodigy is widely used to describe children and young people who have acquired an exceptional degree of knowledge or expertise for their age. However, although that word is a useful label for designating certain very able children, there is no clearly defined category of prodigies. In particular, there is no clear dividing line between children who are definitely prodigies and young people who are unusually able or precocious but not exceptional enough to be called prodigies.

Another complication is that whether people do or do not refer to a child as being a prodigy does not depend only on the degree to which the young person is exceptional. One factor affecting the likelihood of a child being called a prodigy is the degree to which the child's exceptional abilities are ones that are readily apparent. In the case of a child who is a performing musician, for instance, the unusual capabilities are ones that other people can easily become aware of, simply because a musical performance puts skills on display. So it will be fairly obvious that a particular child's accomplishments are well above the average. However, if the child's special expertise or knowledge takes the form of capacities that are not obvious to other people, there will be less likelihood of the child being identified as being unusually able and called a prodigy. For example, when a child's special expertise takes the form of unusual degree of knowledge of history or philosophy, this is unlikely to be widely noticed by others.

Generally speaking, when a number of children are equally exceptional, those whose special capabilities are relatively "public" and are easy to put on display are more likely to be called prodigies than children whose special accomplishments are more private and less obvious to other people. That is one reason why the young Mozart was widely acknowledged be a prodigy whilst the young Einstein was not. Einstein as a child was almost certainly unusually clever, but his special capabilities were not as obvious to other people as Mozart's were.

Contrary to what is widely believed, in most cases there is nothing particularly mysterious about the reasons for children being prodigies. It is not true that some young people become exceptionally able in the absence of any contributing causes. In the majority of cases, when a young person gains skills or knowledge much earlier than is usual, it is because there have been special opportunities to learn or special encouragement. Quite often, a parent will have made special efforts to help the child to learn.

That is not to say that *any* child will become a prodigy if only the parents make enough effort to give encouragement. A large number of contributing influences are involved, including motivation, personality, temperament, and the child's likes and preferences, and inherited sources of individual variability make a contribution. Generally speaking, however, those children whose parents are good at aiding learning by providing stimulation and support, and being sensitive enough to maintain the child's motivation, are especially likely to become prodigies. Becoming a prodigy partly depends on the parents' effectiveness in providing a stimulating and supportive environment, but the way in which the child actually experiences things is even more important, and that is largely outside the parents' control.

The relationship between being a child prodigy and becoming a creative adult

How does being a prodigy affect an individual's chances of being an exceptionally capable adult? Two questions are important here. First, in order to be the kind of adult person who makes creative achievements, is it necessary to have been a prodigy during childhood? Second, if not, does being a prodigy help or hinder a young person's chances of having a successful adult career?

Among exceptionally able and creative adults, a number have either been regarded as prodigies in childhood or have made especially good progress by the end of childhood, but without this being sufficiently noticed by others for the word prodigy to have been applied to them. However, there have been at least a few cases of individuals who were not at all exceptional as children but neverthe-less made outstanding creative achievements in adulthood. Charles Darwin was one such person. His progress at school was never more than average, and although at home he was seen as a bright and lively child, neither his father nor his sisters — who took a close interest in his education — discerned anything remarkable in his mental capacities.

If it is not essential for a creative adult to have been a child prodigy, is it helpful? Sometimes it undoubtedly is. Especially in those areas of expertise where it takes many years to gain essential capabilities, it may be vital to have made considerable progress by the end of child-hood. In music, for instance, in common with other skill areas ranging from sports and performing arts to mathematics and the sciences, for someone who reaches adulthood without having made considerable progress, even finding the time that needs to be devoted to practice and training activities in order to gain essential skills would be extremely difficult. So having been a prodigy would be an advantage, not because there is any vital link between being a prodigy and being an exceptional adult, but because having been a prodigy is an indica-tion of having made a good early start.

However, being a prodigy can also have disadvantages, so far as a child's future is concerned. Quite frequently, a parent will be very heavily involved in the child's training, and in some cases the parent's identification with the child's success can be so extreme as to interfere

with the child's development as an independent and autonomous individual who is capable of making personal decisions. Such a parent may concentrate on encouraging the child to acquire expertise in a particular sphere, at the expense of opportunities to make friends and learn how to get on with other people, and develop the social skills that someone needs in order to enjoy an independent life. So the child may end up having exceptional abilities but lacking other capacities, and without the sense of one's own direction on which a successful and fulfilling career depends. As we have seen, one of the most striking characteristics of adults who make creative achievements is that they do possess a strong sense of purpose and direction. They are also very independent. A young person who grows up under the shadow of an ambitious parent may fail to develop the broader qualities needed in order to enjoy a happy life as an adult.

What is a genius?

When we call someone a genius we are not only acknowledging that the person possesses exceptional creative powers. The fact that we use that term is also an acknowledgement that the individual has succeeded in producing achievements—in art, original thought, science, invention, or some other field of discovery—that have made an enormous impact.

A relatively small number of creative individuals, including Plato, Aristotle, Copernicus, Rembrandt, Shakespeare, Newton, Darwin, Einstein, Mozart, Beethoven, and Darwin, and perhaps fifty or a hundred others have been very widely acknowledged to have been geniuses. A much larger number of individuals, possibly as many as thousands, have been regarded as being geniuses by substantial numbers of people. However, there is no single definition of a genius that is universally accepted, and no agreed way of deciding whether or not a particular individual deserves to be called a genius.

One of the reasons underlying these difficulties is that in saying that a person is a genius one is not really *describing* the person but making a statement about the *impact* of the person's achievements. Geniuses are almost always intelligent, creative, single-minded, and extremely diligent, but even if we possessed excellent ways of measuring all those qualities that would not make it possible to decide whether or not a particular individual was a genius. There are plenty of individuals who possess all these qualities in abundance, but despite being intelligent, creative, and so on, have never produced achievements that have made the major impact that forms a necessary criterion for being regarded as a genius.

To some extent, the impact of a person's achievements is outside the individual's control. How someone's accomplishments are received by others does depend on the person's qualities, but it also depends on outside factors, including luck, fashion, the climate of the times, and on whether or not there happens to be a good match between the person's capabilities and those accomplishments that are valued or needed at the particular time in history. Put simply, with some outstandingly able and creative people, things turn out well, and others acknowledge and respect their achievements. These individuals stand a good chance of being regarded as geniuses. For other people who are just as able, things do not turn out so well. They make less of an impact and nobody calls them geniuses.

It is sometimes thought that genius and its causes are mysterious phenomena, and impossible to explain except by assuming that a person must have been born with some special powers. Indeed, in the past it was widely thought that a person's "genius" was some kind of special force that was partly outside the individual possessing it, in the way that a poet's "muse" has been seen as a power that is separate from the person's normal mental processes. And because the achievements of a genius like Mozart are as dazzling as they are, and so far in excess of what ordinary people can imagine themselves making, it is easy to believe that the origins of those achievements must lie in causes that are also very different from the ones that make more ordinary accomplishments possible.

Nevertheless, there are no convincing reasons for believing that the influences that lead to a person becoming capable of the most creative achievements really are fundamentally different from the causes of achievements that are outstanding but not quite so exceptional. It is more likely that the differences in the contributing factors are largely ones of degree.

Creativity

People who are equally intelligent, skilled, and hard-working may differ enormously in the degree to which they are imaginative, fertile, expressive, or inventive. Some highly able individuals, but not others, are fluent and productive. Some people produce bounteous constructive or original ideas, or copious unique insights. These individuals are said to be highly creative, and their creativity is much valued.

Predictably, attempts have been made to develop ways of measuring a person's creativity, on the assumption that creativity tests can be developed just as can intelligence scales. The idea has been that measures of young people's creativity would make it possible to identify which individuals would be capable of creative achievements. Unfortunately, however, although a number of tests of tests of creativity have been devised, they have not proved to be very effective. A crippling limitation is that none of the tests has been very useful for predicting the extent to which a person will actually make creative achievements.

Are the thinking processes underlying creative achievements fundamentally different from those involved in everyday problem solving? Is creative thinking ever totally original? Can it yield ideas that are entirely unrelated to earlier ones? Surprisingly, perhaps, the answer to all these questions appears to be "No". This is not to deny that there is much that is original or novel in creative thought. But it also seems clear that even the most creative thinking of all builds on previous ideas and makes use of previous knowledge, if only to reject or transform them. Inventions never emerge in a complete void. Even the most creative people build on the past achievements of others. They also depend on training and practice and learn from experience, contradicting the myth that creative inventions spring from nowhere. For instance, as Robert Weisberg (1993) has shown, the view that the Wright brothers, who developed powered flight, were just obscure bicycle makers who worked on flight as a kind of hobby is largely false. In fact, they were not only extremely serious and systematic about what they were doing, but they also went to great lengths to inform

The Wright brothers' plane. Photograph courtesy TRIP, photographer E. Young

themselves about the progress that was being made by other inventors who were attempting to make flight possible.

Summary

The three principles of learning that were first introduced in Chapter 1 all play a part in the acquisition of abilities gained by older children and adults. For example, active approaches to learning are evident in the use of memory aids, learning strategies based on visual imagery, and in note-taking. Repetition plays a key role in the practice and training abilities that lead to high levels of performance at various skills.

Research into expertise has stressed the importance of describing how experts undertake tasks, and comparing experts and non-experts. Individuals who achieve high levels of ability are almost always strongly motivated to succeed, and also depend on having a capacity to maintain their concentration on particular tasks.

High achievers generally do well at intelligence tests, but at the very highest levels of intelligence there is little relationship between a person's test scores and their actual success in making creative achievements. High achievers are often assumed to possess innate talents. However, some research findings appear to contradict the talent account.

Some creative individuals have been exceptionally able even in childhood, prompting others to call them prodigies. However, by no means all prodigies excel as adults. A few very exceptionally creative people are regarded as geniuses. That term is used more as an acknowledgement of a person's contribution than as a description of the person.

Human creativity is much valued, but attempts to assess creativity as a stable attribute of individuals have not been successful, and findings tend to contradict the view that creative kinds of thinking are fundamentally different from other kinds of thinking.

Further reading

Interesting articles on the acquisition of various kinds of expertise are in K.A. Ericsson, (Ed.) (1996), *The road to excellence: The acquisition of expert performance in the arts and sciences, sports and games* (Mahwah, NJ: Lawrence Erlbaum Associates Inc). An excellent introduction to creativity is provided by R.W. Weisberg (1993), *Creativity: Beyond the myth of genius* (New York: Freeman). The acquisition of high abilities is discussed in M.J.A. Howe (1990), *The origins of exceptional abilities* (Oxford: Blackwell).

Becoming a more successful learner

6

Because psychological research has added to our understanding of human learning and abilities, it should be possible to apply what has been discovered to our own daily lives, in ways that benefit our everyday activities as students and learners. This chapter examines ways in which this can be done. We start with a reminder that people's effectiveness as learners and students is affected by broader influences such as motivation and personality. Then we turn to the activity of studying, examining the practices that make someone into a successful learner. Finally, the chapter provides useful information relating to some of the many study skills and activities on which learners depend.

Being more effective

Most people would like to be better learners. In principle this does not seem at all impossible: we would be bound to improve if only we worked a little harder, spent more time studying, and concentrated more closely. Everyone knows that, but it does not seem to help.

Let's examine some of the reasons students and other learners give for not doing as well as they would like to, which will enable some of the most common problems to be identified. Some of those problems may turn out to be illusory, and others may be intractable, but it is usually possible to discover the reasons for someone failing to thrive. And once that is done we can begin to see what needs changing. Here are some comments by a student:

> *For me, learning is too much like hard work. It is not at all relaxing, and I quickly get tired.*

This is quite a common response: there is no denying that learning can be hard work at times. But this in itself should not be a huge obstacle.

After all, many of the activities that people most enjoy involve a great deal of work and effort. Playing football is often hard and tiring, for example. So are many sports and leisure activities. Even dancing can be fatiguing. Generally speaking, the mere fact that an activity demands hard work is not, on its own, enough to put people off. What is more aversive is the *combination* of the need to study hard and other arduous obligations. So, for instance, having to work hard at studying a subject that a person does not find interesting is often aversive. So too is the necessity to study hard when someone is highly anxious and fearful of failure.

There are no easy remedies for dealing with difficulties like these. However, progress some has been made here, simply by establishing that the real problem is not what it initially seemed to be—sheer difficulty—but something more complicated. By identifying the true nature of someone's problem we can often make a large step towards solving it. Once it is established that the real causes of a person's difficulties lie at least partly in negative motivational influences—such as the ones that were explored in Chapter 4—the search for solutions can be more accurately directed, raising the chances of success.

Here is another person's comment:

> I usually get on fine until I come to something I don't understand. But then I panic, and that puts me right off learning and studying.

A number of students find this a cause for concern, and one that makes it hard to enjoy the activity of studying. It is a problem that will be addressed in the present chapter, in the section entitled Reading to learn.

Another frequent concern is evident in the following responses:

> I worry about getting behind, and this makes me anxious.

> What keeps me back is that I can never make up my mind what to study. As soon as I start on one topic I begin to wonder if I shouldn't be doing something else. In the end I don't get anything done.

It is all too easy to fritter away time wondering what to do next, and worrying about failing to make up one's mind is another time-waster. Part of the solution lies in being well organised and making plans in advance. Establishing regular study habits is also helpful. In this chapter we shall examine ways to do this.

A particularly serious concern is evident in the next remark:

> *In principle I'm really keen to learn, but when I get down to it I just can't concentrate.*

This is a depressing state of affairs, especially when someone's inability to concentrate leads to increased anxiety. That makes it even harder to concentrate, raising the person's anxiety level even more. However, there are a few simple principles which, when followed, can help to solve the problem. These include:

(a) break learning tasks down into small parts;
(b) have frequent rests;
(c) engage in activities such as note-taking that help a learner to sustain attention; and
(d) avoid unnecessary distractions.

Yet more negative feelings about studying are expressed in the following remarks:

> *I like doing things with other people. Studying is too solitary for me.*

> *Learning does not bring me any rewards. I don't mind working at something providing there is a satisfying result. But with learning, this doesn't seem to happen.*

Both of these concerns are real enough. To some extent learning is inevitably an activity that people engage in on their own, although working with others and sharing learning experiences can make studying a more social activity.

It is also true that the rewards that learning brings tend not to be immediate ones. All the same, learning can often be made more enjoyable. Just taking a more active role can help. Getting regular feedback about progress is also beneficial. In some circumstances feedback can be gained from regular self-testing, a learning strategy that was outlined in Chapter 1. Sometimes, just taking simple precautions such as having regular pauses from studying and making sure that one is warm and comfortable can make a real difference.

In conclusion

The preceding comments by students illustrate the fact that people do encounter obstacles to learning and studying. There is nothing surprising about that: learning often takes an effort and it is not always fun. As was pointed out in Chapter 1, evolution has not provided humans with brains that are specifically designed for undertaking the kinds of learning challenges that are presented by the modern world.

However, none of the obstacles is insuperable. As we have seen, once it is possible to identify the difficulties that are getting in the way of learning, it is usually possible to take steps that will reduce or eliminate them.

The value of organising one's time and activities

In most aspects of life, people are most likely to succeed at getting things done when they are reasonably well organised. A person who has an organised routine finds it easier to get on with the jobs that need doing in a down-to-earth and effective manner. Such a person will usually know what has to be achieved at any particular time.

Someone who is disorganised, in contrast, will be less effective. That person is likely to waste time fretting about other things rather than concentrating on the task at hand, and switching from one job to another before the first is finished. Disorganised people keep having to decide what to do. They frequently change their minds and worry about whether the right decision has been made.

As was pointed out in Chapter 4, to some extent achieving the kind of self-organisation that allows people to get on with the jobs they need to do is a consequence of acquiring regular habits. Doing so makes it easier to get routine tasks finished. Most people wash themselves and get dressed every morning, for example, and they do not find that difficult. It is not that there is anything particularly interesting or enjoyable about these tasks, but it is easy to do them simply because a firm habit has been acquired. Because they have established firm habits, the majority of adults do not fritter away time every morning agonising about whether or not to brush their teeth.

With learning and studying, the benefits to an individual of being well organised are just as substantial as they are with any other kind of activity. By and large, the organised learner is an effective learner. This message is not one that is universally welcomed. Understandably,

people, perhaps especially when they are young, like to think of themselves as free spirits, so far as learning and education are concerned. We want to preserve the excitement and spontaneity of learning new skills and adding to what we know, and we place value on the spirit of discovery. Seen in that light, the idea of regarding studying as being just a task like any other task seems somewhat unromantic and decidedly unglamorous. More organisation seems to mean less spontaneity, and less freedom to follow one's own interests and impulses.

Yet there is no escaping the fact that being well organised does make people more productive and more effective. This is just as true of learning and study activities as it is of any other areas of daily life. Successful learners get on with the tasks they have set for themselves, and consequently they manage to get things completed. Learners who delay studying until they feel "in the mood" and then try to decide how to spend their time rarely have much success in the long run.

For students especially, one reason why it is important to impose a degree of self-organisation on learning and studying is that these activities lack some of the built-in organisation and structure that are present in the everyday lives of most people who work at paid jobs. If you are working as a waitress, for example, it is fairly clear what has to be done, and when to do it: your activities at any time are largely structured by the demands of the job. For most full-time students, in contrast, the daily routine is not so constrained. There are more decision points where a choice ("What shall I do now?") has to be made. Consequently, students do have to be *self*-organised, and impose their own structure on their activities to a greater extent than is usually necessary in paid jobs. Being well organised as a student has a number of aspects:

1. It is partly a matter of making good advance plans. In writing an essay, for example, in order to do the work efficiently it is helpful to decide in advance what has to be done and when to do it. It will also be useful to ensure that the information and other materials needed will be available when they are required.
2. It is also necessary to decide the order in which tasks should be attempted. A student who is struggling to complete a number of assignments can waste a lot of time worrying about that rather than actually getting on with the work that needs doing. It is important to be able to prioritise. Making a list of what has to be done and deciding on the order in which each item has to be completed can reduce uncertainty and the

anxiety that it creates. Once an ordered list of tasks has been made, a student can concentrate on doing what needs to be done, one item at a time.

3. Helpful structuring of one's work is often achieved simply by dividing a large task into a number of smaller ones. Take essays, for example. The prospect of writing a long essay may seem dauntingly unmanageable. But once that task has been divided into smaller stages, for instance by making sensible advance plans that involve dividing up the proposed essay into a number of parts, the project becomes a much more manageable one. It has now become a matter of doing a number of medium-sized tasks, and each of these can be completed within a reasonable amount of time.

Making and using a timetable

Being well organised is largely a matter of managing one's *time* effectively. The easiest way of doing this is by making a timetable and keeping to it. Timetables save people wasted time and effort in a number of ways. In particular, they cut down on the necessity to keep making decisions about what to do. As a result, far less energy is wasted on worrying about making good choices.

There is nothing difficult about devising a timetable for oneself: doing so is largely a matter of common sense. However, there are a few non-obvious points that need to be taken into account. In particular, there are some common errors that need to be avoided:

- A common mistake is to devise a timetable that is too demanding. This sometimes happens because a person's decision to make a timetable coincides with their deciding to study harder. Don't let your enthusiasm carry you away! It is not a good idea to introduce a timetable and make drastic lifestyle changes at exactly the same time. When you decide to change your study habits it is usually best to do so by a series of small and gradual changes, rather than a sudden huge alteration that you may not be able to sustain.

- Make sure that you allow plenty of time for your non-work activities, including meals, necessary travelling time, and leisure. Avoid making your timetable too rigid. Don't think of establishing a timetable as a way of sentencing yourself to a regime of hard labour! The timetable is your assistant, not your master: if you find your timetable more of a constraint rather than a help, it is not doing its job properly. There needs to be a degree of flexibility.

- All the same, once you have made your timetable do keep to it when possible. Don't keep asking yourself if you feel like doing the task you have set yourself, or if you are in the mood for it: just do it! The more you get into the habit of getting on with what needs to be done, whether or not that is what you feel you especially want to do, the easier it becomes.

- If you have definitely decided to extend your working week, do so gradually. For example, if you are starting to study on Sundays for the first time, begin with just an hour or so. Remember, everyone needs some time off.

- Don't have long study periods without making provision for reasonably frequent breaks in which you can stop working and enjoy a rest and a cup of coffee.

- Even short study sessions can be valuable. A period of as little as 15 minutes can make a difference. A session as short as that might not be very useful for making progress on an essay, because for that you will need time to collect materials together and get started, but for a reading task a concentrated quarter-hour of study can make a real difference.

- Plan to do your most difficult study tasks at times when you normally feel wide awake and alert.

- You need to strike a balance between feeling that you must never ever depart from your timetable, and frequently ignoring it. An ideal timetable is one that you can comfortably keep to almost all the time, except in emergencies.

- If you have not used a timetable previously, the first one you design will probably turn out to be less than ideal. Don't be surprised if this happens, and avoid the temptation to abandon having a timetable altogether. The chances are that a few simple revisions are all that is needed.

Reading to learn

Almost everyone can read and for most people reading is one of the main ways in which they learn, especially in connection with the acquisition of knowledge and understanding. Nevertheless, even successful learners often feel less than confident about their capacity to learn from reading. Students sometimes report feeling more secure when information is conveyed by the human voice, as happens in lectures and classes, or when radio or television are involved.

It is a great pity that so many individuals are not happy to learn from the written word alone, because writing has a number of strong advantages over all other ways of communicating knowledge. For instance, compared with what is involved in attending a lecture or a class, students who have the same material to learn from in written form:

Photograph courtesy TRIP, photographer R. Chester

- do not have to travel to a particular place at a particular time to have access to the information;
- can go through the information at their own pace;
- can skip any information that has previously been learned and can repeatedly read unfamiliar material that is too difficult to understand at first reading;
- can test themselves, and get immediate feedback by checking to see whether they are correct; and
- can underline important points, or make notes, without the danger of missing important information that is present when material is presented via a class or lecture.

In a word, people who learn through reading are more *independent* as learners. They do not have to depend on teachers and lecturers. Students for whom reading is the main source of information learn at their own convenience. They are able to progress at their own pace, and can do their learning when, where, and how it best suits them. Reading is in many circumstances the most flexible learning activity of all, and also the one that is most likely to help students to be independent. It gives people the power to extend their knowledge of what they need to know even when no teacher or lecturer is available to provide assistance. Consequently, any person who has got into the habit of using reading as a major source of input for learning activities has gained a number of real advantages.

Recognising the value of reading does not mean denying that lectures can sometimes be an especially helpful or stimulating way of providing information. Nor does it mean forgetting that there are numerous other ways in which teachers can help students to learn. But, at least in connection with the function of imparting the informa-

Photograph
courtesy TRIP,
photographer H.
Rogers

tion that a learner needs to acquire, the huge advantages of reading do need to be acknowledged. Reading really does liberate the learner.

Why do some people find it difficult to learn through reading?

It is worth asking why it is that so many students find it so difficult to learn from reading. It is then worth looking for ways to reduce their difficulties. We start with a description by a student, Richard, of the experience of reading:

> *The teacher told us to read this chapter. It is 30 pages long. When I started it I was taking notes, but that meant it took twenty minutes to get to the end of the first page and I only had an hour or so for the whole chapter. So I stopped taking notes. After a couple more pages I got a bit bored: I couldn't see where the chapter was going and much of the information was fairly familiar. So I sort of drifted off, and when I reached page six I realised I could not remember anything from the page before. About that time I also found that I just could not understand what the author was saying, it was just too difficult, so I gave up.*

Sounds familiar? There are very few students who have never experienced some of these problems. We shall look at them in turn, and discover how and why Richard was going wrong.

1. A first warning sign in the description quoted is provided by the fact that although the chapter is rather a long one—30 pages—Richard did not make any plans prior to starting it. It would have been sensible to begin by taking a look at the chapter's overall structure, and gaining a broad preliminary understanding of the aims of the chapter and the manner in which it was organised. Having done that, the next step might have been to make an intermediate goal of completing the first part of the chapter. More often than not, a 30-page chapter will be too long to complete at one sitting, especially if the reader finds the content at all difficult. In fact, the chances of someone reading and fully understanding a chapter that long in one hour, let alone remembering a substantial part of its content, are rather slim. So, having gained a knowledge of the chapter's main aims and structure, Richard might have been wise to think about how much of it could be mastered in the time available, rather than simply starting to read without making any plans at all.

2. Richard tells us that he first became aware of a specific problem when he discovered that his progress was too slow, because so much of his time was being spent making notes. Here again, it is clear that the absence of any advance planning was a contributing factor. At an early stage a decision about note-taking should have been made. Making detailed notes can be a very helpful activity (as we saw in Chapter 5) and may aid learning considerably, but it does take a substantial amount of time. Taking very brief notes, which demands less time,

may have been sufficient for Richard's needs. To complicate matters slightly, it may not have been possible to make a wise decision about how much time to spend on making notes until it became clear what the chapter contained, and how difficult it was, and how unfamiliar, or until Richard knew how much of the detailed information in the chapter had to be learned. Perhaps Richard needed to make detailed notes on some of the chapter's contents, but only brief notes, or none at all, on parts of the chapter that were less crucial. In any case, more than one reading of the chapter would have been necessary. It is entirely possible that it would not have become clear to Richard what kinds of notes were going to be necessary until a first reading had been completed.

3. The next obstacle Richard encountered was the fact that he became bored. How could he have avoided this? One solution might have been to skip or merely skim those parts of the material that he found were already familiar. However, because he had not taken the trouble to look at the overall structure in advance, he had no way of telling whether or not that would have been a wise move. It is quite likely that the passivity of Richard's approach to reading the chapter after he had stopped taking notes contributed to his experiencing boredom. As we have seen, there are various activities, ranging from taking a few brief notes or underlining important words, to self-testing, that would have reduced the likelihood of boredom by making Richard's role a more active one.

4. The final problem — and the one that prompted Richard to give up entirely — was that the reading simply got too difficult. Recall that at one point he found that he just could not understand the material. Sheer difficulty is an important obstacle, of course, and one that is not uncommon. So it is important to know how to overcome it. What can learners do when they discover that they are failing to understand the material they are reading? Here are some useful suggestions:

- Don't panic, but simply slow down. That advice may sound obvious, but it is surprising how many learners fail to adjust their reading rate according to the difficulty of the material. One reason is that most readers have got into the habit of reading at a certain pace, which is usually the reading speed that works best with most of the materials that the individual reads. If the majority of our reading involves, say, newspapers or novels, we tend to go on reading at the same rate that we use for those kinds of materials even when we are reading something very different. In reality, however, with denser or more difficult material, which may involve longer words, more complex sentences, abstract ideas, and information that is not at all familiar, it may be necessary to slow down considerably, simply because there is so much more to take in.

Perceiving the desirability of slowing down one's reading rate and actually doing so are not the same thing, of course. It will require a conscious effort, but it is certainly worth making the attempt. With difficult and unfamiliar materials, failures to understand what is being read are almost inevitable unless the reader is prepared to slow down.

- Stop briefly at the end of each sentence and check that you have understood it. If you are not sure, read it again. Doing this is a good way to avoid the not uncommon experience in which a reader discovers that not only has the most recent sentence or two not been fully understood, but neither has a large proportion of the content of the last page. If you find yourself in that situation the only solution is to go right back to the last point that you did read with full understanding.

- When you reach a point at which you feel yourself failing to understand what you are reading, carefully identify exactly what it is that you do not understand. As in many aspects of life, until you have identified precisely what the problem is, it is unlikely that you will be able to fix it. And conversely, once you have put your finger on the precise problem, solving it may be a lot easier than you expect. Even if you seek assistance from a teacher or lecturer, it is unlikely that they will be able to do much to help you unless you have taken the trouble to sort out precisely what it is that you need to know.

- Not knowing the meaning of a particular word or technical term is a common source of difficulty. If you come across a word you don't know, look it up.

- Keep monitoring your understanding. Trying to write down a sentence in your own words is one good way of checking whether you have really understood it. Regular self-testing is another useful way of monitoring your progress.

- Finally, you should be aware that even the most capable and successful individuals sometimes have to read a passage three or more times in order to understand it properly. So if you do not get the full meaning at the first or second pass there is no need to get discouraged. It does not mean you are stupid, or failing. Just keep trying. Refuse to be defeated. That's a strategy that has worked for many highly successful people, including Isaac Newton and a number of other geniuses. It will usually work for you, too!

Writing

Do you find writing difficult? If you do, join the club! Surprisingly few people find writing easy. Writing *is* difficult. It is particularly hard when one is struggling to express complicated or abstract ideas.

Something that many learners find especially frustrating about writing is that unlike many skills it does not seem to get much easier with experience. There is a reason for that perception, which is that the older and more sophisticated writer is typically trying to achieve more. In reality, as we mature as learners, our ability to express ourselves in writing does improve considerably, even if it does not always feel like that.

Why is it so much harder to communicate in writing than in speech? The main reason is that with face-to-face communicating through talk, unlike writing, there are numerous things that we can do to help the communication process. People can introduce facial expressions and gestures, for example, and raise or lower their voices. Listeners can nod their heads to indicate agreement or shake their heads to show disagreement or disbelief. Talkers can explicitly request feedback by inserting phrases such as "Do you know what I mean?" or "Is that clear?" People can repeat themselves when unsure that their messages have been understood. Listeners can ask for repetition ("Say that again.") or reassurance ("Are you really telling me that...").

In short, there is a range of devices that talkers can introduce in order to become less exclusively dependent on the words that convey their messages. In everyday conversations we constantly rely on these aids. We usually take them for granted, and only become aware of their importance at times when they are unavailable. This happens, for instance, when it is necessary to convey a message to an answering machine, a situation that often leaves people tongue-tied until they get used to it. Having to talk to an answering machine is not entirely unlike having to communicate through writing. In both of these situations, unlike spoken conversations, the message has to be absolutely lucid. There is no one to let us know if we have forgotten a crucial part of the message, or to point out that its meaning is not entirely clear.

With writing—as with addressing an answering machine—because everything depends on the words of the message, it is vital for the meaning of the communication to be clear. To a considerable extent this is achieved by the writer being careful to follow those rules that make language "grammatical". Grammatical language is, essentially, language that obeys certain structural rules. These rules help to ensure that the message is not ambiguous, and that the meaning received by the recipient of the message is the same as the one intended by the sender. It is because of the role grammar plays in achieving that end that it is so crucial in written language. As we have seen, grammar is less important in spoken language, because when people talk to one another they can call on other devices (which are unavailable for writers) for helping to ensure that the recipient actually receives and understands the intended message.

Grammatical written language is not always meaningful, but as a rule the intended meaning of a written communication that follows the rules of grammar is likely to be clear. Conversely, the meaning of writing that does not obey grammatical rules is not likely to be at all clear.

Ways to improve writing skills

In an ideal world all pupils would leave school equipped to express themselves clearly in writing. In reality, many school leavers fall short of being able to do so. What can be done to improve one's own ability to write in grammatical English?

Gaining the capability to write well involves acquiring a number of skills, and it would be foolish to assume that competence at writing can be quickly or easily achieved. A comprehensive course of instruction on how to write will inevitably involve considerable length and detail. For readers who feel the need for substantial assistance with writing, I particularly recommend Andrew Northedge's *The good study guide* (Open University, 1990). The aim of the remaining part of the present section will be the more modest one of providing some useful hints and advice about effective writing. Here are some pointers that many students find helpful:

1. Most important of all, it is necessary to be able to tell the difference between grammatical and ungrammatical writing. There are two kinds of learning experience that will help a student to do this. The first is the experience of learning the formal grammar that is taught in schools. The other is through regularly reading the output of competent writers. Good writing can be found in many places, including newspapers and magazines as well as books. Perhaps surprisingly, even in tabloid newspapers grammatical standards are usually high.

People who are frequent readers become good at telling the difference between grammatical and ungrammatical writing. Regular reading also exposes readers to examples of effective *styles* of writing. Writing style is an elusive concept, not so easily pinned down as grammar. It refers to ways in which a writer creates distinctiveness and elegance in writing. Whereas grammatical writing is achieved by following clear rules, style is a more subtle matter of making written messages effective by the use of a number of devices, including rhythm, good phrasing, and careful choice of words.

2. Like other skills, the ability to write well cannot be acquired unless there are plenty of opportunities to practise writing. The more writing you do, the better, irrespective of whether it takes the form of essays, book reviews, practical reports, fiction, poetry, or even personal letters. The majority of well known authors have been enthusiastic and active writers throughout their lives. The Brontë sisters, for example, were constantly writing stories even when they were children, and they always maintained the habit of writing.

3. Except when the content of a communication is simple or familiar, even the best writers will need to work through a number of drafts in order to produce good writing. Finding the right word, or the best way to phrase a message, may take a number of attempts. That fluent and elegantly expressed column you admire in your newspaper may give the impression of having flowed easily from the journalist's mind, but in reality it is more likely to be the end-product of a long and difficult writing process that involved a succession of repeatedly revised versions. Good writers rarely expect their first draft to be satisfactory, and expert writers spend more time revising their work than non-experts do (Hayes & Flower, 1986).

Good writers acquire expertise at detecting the shortcomings in their early drafts. They are prepared to keep revising their work, a process that may involve producing half a dozen successive versions, until a satisfactory one is achieved. Compared with less skilled writers, experts are better at perceiving the mistakes in an early version. When making revisions, experts are more likely than less capable writers to change the whole structure of a sentence rather than just amending individual words. To write well, a combination of ability to see the faults in one's output and willingness to keep working at improving the work is essential.

4. Perhaps the most common fault in inadequate student writing is that it contains strings of words that do not form genuine sentences. The defect often takes the form of the absence of a main verb. Without this, even the longest stream of words will never make a sentence. Thus while "Jesus wept" is an acceptable sentence, "having walked from one end of the globe to another, a journey which took many years of hardship, during which James changed from being a healthy young man to a shadow of his former self" is not. It is not uncommon to discover non-sentences in a first draft, but people all too often fail to spot these errors when reading through their own work. It is definitely worth making an effort to eliminate non-sentences, as their meaning is often unclear.

5. There is nothing wrong with short sentences. Some people appear to believe that a writer who produces short sentences will be seen as simple-minded or naive, but there are no genuine grounds for this view. Even the shortest sentences can be highly effective. Although it is true that a passage composed *entirely* of short sentences may give an impression of lack of sophistication, there is no reason to suppose that long sentences are more desirable than short ones. Generally speaking, the longer a sentence is, the more opportunities arise for mismatches between the meaning intended by the writer and the one actually perceived by the reader.

6. A practice that should be avoided in writing involves connecting two separate short sentences with a comma, to make one longer sentence, as in "Fred kicked Arthur, the cat slept on the ground". Here we have two separate ideas, "Fred kicked Arthur" and "the cat slept on the ground". Each justifies a sentence of its own. Had there been some clear relationship between the ideas it would have been permissible to join them by a colon, making one sentence, as in "Jack fell down and broke his crown: his friend came running after". However, it would be equally permissible to have two separate sentences here, and it would definitely not be correct to join the two ideas into one sentence with no more than a comma to separate them.

7. Always write in paragraphs. For readers, paragraphs break up a long stream of text into manageable "bites", corresponding with the separate points the author is making. Paragraph length can vary enormously, but when a paragraph exceeds about 10 sentences the chances are that the information will be

easier for a reader to comprehend if the content is divided into two shorter paragraphs.

It is permissible to have some paragraphs that contain only one or two sentences. However, if all your paragraphs are that short it is likely that the narrative will appear to be disjointed. Broadly speaking, the time to start a new paragraph is when you have finished making one point and are moving on to something different.

8. Be sparing in your use of pronouns such as "it", "this" and "that", "these", and "they". Such words should only be used when it is clear what they refer to. When it is not, the meaning of a passage is likely to be obscure. Consider, for instance the following passage from a recent scientific book:

> Even those who have long denied that genes say much about human existence are (often grudgingly) accepting that they can at least set the limits within which it is lived.

In this sentence there is not much doubt about the final "it", which can only refer to "human existence". But what about the earlier "they" (in "they can at least...")? Does that pronoun refer to the people who have denied, or does it refer to the genes? On reflection, "they" probably refers to the genes, but the momentary uncertainty, even if soon dispelled, may impede understanding.

9. Spelling is important. It could be argued that examiners and teachers sometimes place too much stress on the value of correct spelling. Nevertheless good spelling is usually considered to be a necessary element of competent writing.

Some poor spellers believe, usually incorrectly, that their spelling simply cannot be improved. The fact that even people who are frequent readers can be very poor spellers may contribute to this mistaken belief. In reality, because the reading process for experienced readers is a partly automatic one, in which little attention is given to the single letters that comprise a word, it is not at all surprising that certain enthusiastic and highly competent readers happen to be poor spellers.

Spelling is a skill like any other skill. It can be improved through deliberate training and practice. Frequent use of a dictionary is helpful, especially in conjunction with deliberate rehearsal of a word that has just been looked up. Short cuts to

good spelling can be gained by memorising certain spelling rules, which can be found in some dictionaries and "how to spell" books. There are exceptions to most rules of spelling, of course, but a knowledge of the rules will usually elicit the correct spelling of a word.

Studying for examinations

In many respects, the kinds of learning activities that go into studying for an exam are no different from the day-to-day learning experiences that enable people to gain new knowledge and extend their skills. The same activities are helpful, such as making plans and organising one's time efficiently. There is one vital difference, however. As an examination approaches, the particular capabilities that help learners to make effective use of their competence under specific exam circumstances become increasingly crucial.

Exam room at Sacred Heart School, Amritsar, India. Photograph courtesy TRIP, photographer H. Rogers

It is possible to be well informed about a topic but unable to access one's knowledge quickly and directly. However, it is necessary to do so in order to perform well at an exam. For example, a student who has enjoyed reading a thought-provoking book about a historical period may have learned a great deal about that period, but may not have gained the ability to locate the newly acquired information in the quick and efficient manner that makes it possible to answer examination questions. Here, although reading the book may have been a genuinely educational and enriching experience, and one that has led to increased understanding and knowledge, the learner lacks certain specific capabilities that contribute to exam performance.

In short, doing well at exams demands particular kinds of competence that even good learners sometimes fail to acquire. In an examination it is necessary to have specific facts at one's fingertips. It may be essential to be able to list particular items of information that are relevant to an issue, or to provide examples that illustrate a point, or research findings that support a theory. Someone may be well informed about a topic and have a good general understanding of it, and yet be unable to supply needed details quickly under examination conditions.

The remedy is simple. In a nutshell, it is to have plenty of practice at answering actual examination questions in conditions that are similar to the ones in which the real exam will be taken. It is especially important to gain experience at attempting to provide answers in the allotted time. One's first attempts to do this will be valuable even if they do no more than demonstrate that doing well at an exam takes more than having a vague understanding of some topic that is at the back of one's mind. What you need for an examination is knowledge that is well organised and easily retrieved. Practising answering exam questions is the only sure way to make certain that what you know can be located at the time you need it.

Summary

For a number of reasons students' efforts to learn are not always as effective as they could be. Broad motivational and personality influences can be especially important. This chapter provides practical information about ways to make study activities increasingly effective.

The capacity to organise one's time and activities is a necessary ingredient of success as a learner. This is largely a matter of effective planning and structuring. A timetable can be especially helpful.

Reading frequently provides a vehicle for acquiring new knowledge. It has advantages over other ways of gaining information, and there are a number of steps by which students can increase their effectiveness at reading to learn.

Writing can present difficulties, which are overcome in a variety of ways including an improved knowledge of grammar and spelling, and producing several drafts of a piece of work.

Studying for examinations is more effective when the learner concentrates on activities that ensure that knowledge and skills are readily retrieved in the particular circumstances of taking an examination.

Further reading

A. Northedge (1990), *The good study guide* (Milton Keynes, UK: Open University) provides comprehensive advice about studying.

Glossary

Accelerated learning: learning that involves individuals making unusual early progress as a result of being given special encouragement or learning opportunities.

Achievement motivation: motivational influences related to the fact that performance at many kinds of tasks is affected by the extent to which a person desires to do well.

Advance organiser: information that is provided in order to aid learning by bridging the gap between new or unfamiliar information and the learner's existing knowledge.

Analogies in learning to read: a learner profits from identifying similarities between new words and ones that are already familiar. For example, a child who sees the word *hate* for the first time, but already knows *gate* and *rate*, can deduce the sound of the new item.

Classical conditioning: a simple form of learning, available to many animals as well as humans, in which a response that was originally made to one kind of event comes to be elicited by a new event, as a result of that event being repeatedly paired with the original one. For example, if a newborn baby hears the same sound each time she starts receiving milk, the sucking action that was at first produced only by the stimulus of the milk eventually comes to be elicited also by the sound on its own, even when no milk is provided.

Context: the situation or circumstance in which an event takes place. The particular context in which a person attempts a task can make a great difference to the level of performance.

Correlation: a quantitative indication of the degree of relationship between two factors or dimensions. It is important to be aware that just because two phenomena are correlated does not necessarily mean that there is any cause-and-effect relationship between them.

Creativity: the capacity to produce achievements that are original, imaginative, expressive, or inventive.

Deprivation: in respect to learning, a child is said to have been deprived if adult attention and opportunities to learn have been in short supply.

Expertise: research on expertise aims to understand the detailed nature of the various skills and capabilities that are possessed by an expert in a particular field of ability. This knowledge makes it possible to help other people to become experts.

Extrinsic motivation: motivation that springs from external rewards or incentives, such as money or the approval of other people.

Fear of failure: a negative motivational influence in which anxiety about possible failure impedes an individual from making the effort that is necessary for success.

Fear of success: a state of affairs in which people are held back by their awareness of the fact that succeeding can produce real difficulties for them.

Genetic causation: this term refers to the contribution of inherited information to the form and nature of an individual person.

Genius: this word is introduced in order to acknowledge a person whose exceptional creative achievements have had an enormous impact. It is important to note that there is no straightforward way of defining or measuring genius except in relation to the impact of a person's contributions.

Habituation: although a child normally responds to the first presentation of a new stimulus, the more the stimulus is repeated the less likely it is to produce a reaction. This is useful as a way of enabling an infant or child to react selectively to new or unexpected events, because these events are especially likely to be important ones. Researchers investigating perception make use of habituation as a way of discovering whether a stimulus is perceived as being new.

Head Start: a term designating a large number of programmes, of varying quality and duration, that were designed to provide compensatory early educational experiences to young children considered likely to fail at school as a result of being brought up in a home environment lacking in learning opportunities.

Hothouse: this word is used when young children grow up in circumstances in which learning experiences and expectations are unusually intense.

Imitative learning: learning that involves extending an individual's repertoire of acquired skills by imitating the actions of others.

Incentives: rewards, which can be of many kinds.

Innate gifts and talents: a common view is that certain special inborn qualities are necessary if an individual is to reach the highest levels of achievement in a particular area of competence. Some researchers have disputed this view.

Instinctive behaviour: inherent behaviour that is "built-in" and does not have to be acquired through learning.

Intelligent Quotient (IQ): A broad indication of a person's general intelligence, based on test scores. The average score is 100.

Intrinsic motivation: motivation stemming from internal rewards, such as interest in a task, curiosity, and the enjoyment of doing an activity for its own sake.

Keyword method: a memory aid or **mnemonic** in which the use of visual imagery forms part of a strategy that is intended to make it easier to recall the meaning of words in a foreign language.

Learned helplessness: animals deprived of any effective control over what happens them become unable to learn or function in a normal manner. It appears that similar causes contribute to people becoming passive and indecisive.

Locus of control: a term referring to the fact that people differ in the extent to which they perceive the causes of their successes and failures as being under their own control. A person who sees their locus of control as being largely internal will assume that what they achieve is largely a consequence of their own actions. Someone who perceives control as being external thinks that how well they do is largely out of their hands, and depends on influences such as luck and fate, innate talents, and the influence of other people.

Look and say: an aspect of learning to read in which the learner identifies particular words. This complements **phonics**, in which words are decoded through a knowledge of the rules of letter–sound relationships. Both phonics and look and say play a part in learning to read.

Memory aid: a device or strategy intended to make it easier to remember information. Some memory aids incorporate visual imagery. Others involve ways of creating connections between unrelated items making them more memorable, or other strategies.

Mental state: a term referring to an individual's state of mind. This can vary in different ways, such as mood and state of alertness, with implications for learning and behaviour.

Metaphor: a figure of speech that aids communication by transforming information into a more familiar or concrete form. For example, an incompletely formed idea may be described as "half-baked".

Mnemonic: a memory aid. Some mnemonics make involve making visual images of items to be remembered. With another kind, known as "first-letter mnemonics", the strategy is to provide an easily recalled sentence in which the first letter in each word provides a cue for information that needs to be remembered.

Note-taking: the activity of taking notes provides a useful habit for learners because it creates a convenient record of needed information in a form that makes sense to the individual, at the same time as ensuring that the learner is mentally active.

Numeracy: an understanding of numbers and their relationships.

Operant conditioning: a kind of learning that depends on the fact that the frequency of responses that are reliably rewarded tends to increase. Consequently, behaviour can be altered by selectively rewarding certain actions.

Phonics: an aspect of learning to read that involves the learner acquiring the rules identifying how a word sounds. Phonics enables a learner to decode written language.

Precocity: gaining abilities at a younger age than is usual.

Prodigy: a child or young person who has gained an exceptional degree of knowledge or expertise for their age.

Psychometrics: the branch of science in which attempts are made to measure psychological characteristics.

Reflex: a simple unlearned action that is controlled by inborn or instinctive mechanisms. Babies are born with certain reflex capabilities, such as sucking.

Reinforcers: events that function as rewards, having the effect of increasing the likelihood and frequency of activities that they reliably follow.

Socioeconomic status: an indication of social class in the home background, taking into account standard of living and the level of education received by family members.

Stimulus: in psychology the word usually refers to an event that is presented to an individual as part of an experiment on, say, learning or perception.

Structured home background: an environment in which a child can count on support, dependable people, and clear rules and expectations. These elements have been found to be necessary, in addition to stimulation, for a young person to acquire good **study habits** by the end of childhood.

Study habits: the acquisition of regular habits of learning or studying makes it easier for people to get on with productive activities and diminishes the time wasted by indecision, daydreaming, or inability to concentrate.

Sucking response: one of the behaviours that is seen in newborns. It has obvious survival value, and infants soon learn to vary their sucking behaviour when it is rewarding to do so.

Transfer: the degree to which learning or training involving one skill affects performance at another skill. Generally speaking, transfer only occurs when there are elements in common between the different skills.

Verbal ability: the capacity to solve problems and do tasks that involve the use of language.

References

Amabile, T.M. (1983). *The social psychology of creativity*. NewYork: Springer-Verlag.

Anderson, J.R. (1995). *Cognitive psychology and its implications*. New York: Freeman.

Atkinson, R.C. (1975). Mnemotechnics in second-language learning. *American Psychologist, 30*, 821–828.

Ausubel, D.P. (1968). *Educational psychology: A cognitive view*. New York: Holt, Rinehart, & Winston.

Baltes, P. & Reinert, G. (1969). Cohort effects in cognitive development in children as revealed by cross-sectional sequences. *Developmental Psychology, 1*, 169–177.

Bandura, A. (1986). *Social foundations of thought and action*. Englewood Cliffs, NJ: Prentice Hall.

Bower, G.H., & Clark, M.C. (1969). Narrative stories as mediators of serial learning. *Psychonomic Science, 14*, 181–182.

Bransford, J.D., Nitsch, K.E., & Franks, J.J. (1977). Schooling and the facilitation of knowing. In R.C. Anderson, R.J. Spiro, & W.E. Montague (Eds.), *Schooling and the acquisition of knowledge*. Hillsdale, NJ: Lawrence Erlbaum Associates Inc.

Bransford, J.D., Stein, B.S., Shelton, T.S., & Owings, R.A. (1981). Cognition and adaptation: The importance of learning to learn. In J.H. Farvey (Ed.), *Cognition, social behavior, and the environment*. Hillsdale, NJ: Lawrence Erlbaum Associates Inc.

Brodie, F.M. (1971). *The devil drives: A life of Sir Richard Burton*. Harmondsworth, UK: Penguin.

Bryant, P., & Bradley, L. (1985). *Children's reading problems: Psychology and education*. Oxford: Blackwell.

Ceci, S.J. (1990). *On intelligence...more or less: A bio-ecological treatise on intellectual development*. Englewood Cliffs, NJ: Prentice Hall.

Ceci, S.J., & Bronfenbrenner, U. (1985). Don't forget to take the cupcakes out of the oven: Strategic time-monitoring, prospective memory, and context. *Child Development, 56*, 175–190.

Ceci, S.J., & Liker, J. (1986). A day at the races: A study of IQ, expertise, and cognitive complexity. *Journal of Experimental Psychology: General, 115*, 255–266.

Chase, W.G., & Ericsson, K.A. (1981). Skilled memory. In J.R. Anderson (Ed.), *Cognitive skills and their acquisition*. Hillsdale, NJ: Lawrence Erlbaum Associates Inc.

Cloward, R.D. (1967). Studies in tutoring. *Journal of Experimental Education, 36*, 14–25.

Collier, G. (1994). *Social origins of mental ability*. New York: Wiley.

Csikszentmihalyi, M., & Csikszentmihalyi, I. S. (1993). Family influences on the development of giftedness. In G.R. Bock, & K. Ackrill (Eds.), *CIBA Foundation Symposium No 178: The origins and development of high ability*. Chichester, UK: Wiley.

Csikszentmihalyi, M. Rathunde, K., & Whalen, S. (1993). *Talented teachers: The roots of success and failure*. New York: Cambridge University Press.

Covington, M.L., & Omelich, C.L. (1981). As failures mount: Affective and cognitive consequences of ability demotion in the classroom. *Journal of Educational Psychology, 97*, 149–154.

Darwin, C. (1958). *The autobiography of Charles Darwin, 1809–1822, with original omissions restored.* (Edited with appendix and notes by his grand-daughter Norma Barlow.) London: Collins.

Davies, G.M. (1988). Faces and places: Laboratory research on context and face recognition. In G.M. Davies & D.M. Thomson (Eds.), *Memory in context: Context in memory.* Chichester, UK: Wiley.

de Charms, R. (1976). *Enhancing motivation: Change in the classroom.* New York: Halsted.

Dennis, M., & Dennis, M.G. (1951). Development under controlled environmental conditions. In W. Dennis (Ed.), *Readings in child psychology.* New York: Prentice Hall.

Duchastel, P.C. (1982). Testing effects measured with alternate test forms. *Educational Research, 75,* 309–313.

Durkin, H. (1995). *Developmental social psychology.* Oxford: Blackwell.

Eich, J.E. (1981). The cue-dependent nature of state-dependent retrieval. *Memory and Cognition, 12,* 105–111.

Engen, T., Lipsitt, L.P., & Kaye, H. (1963). Olfactory responses and adaptation in the human neonate. *Journal of Comparative and Physiological Psychology, 56,* 73–77.

Ericsson, K.A. (Ed.) (1996). *The road to excellence: The acquisition of expert performance in the arts and sciences, sports and games.* Mahwah, NJ: Lawrence Erlbaum Associates Inc.

Ericsson, K.A., & Faivre, I.A. (1988). What's exceptional about exceptional abilities? In L.K. Obler & D. Fein (Eds.), *The exceptional brain.* New York: Guilford Press.

Flavell, J.H., Beach, D.R., & Chinsky, J.M. (1966). Spontaneous verbal rehearsal in a memory task as a function of age. *Child Development, 37,* 324–340.

Fowler, W. (1983). *Potentials of childhood. Volume 1: A historical view of early experience.* Lexington, MA: Heath.

Fowler, W., Ogston, K., Roberts, G., Stean, D., & Swenson, A. (1983). *Potentials of childhood. Volume 2: Studies in early developmental learning.* Lexington, MA: Heath.

Fowler, W., Ogston, K., Roberts-Fiati, G., & Swenson, A. (1993). Accelerating language acquisition. In G.R. Bock & K. Ackrill (Eds.), *CIBA Foundation Symposium No 178: The origins and development of high ability.* Chichester, UK: Wiley.

Flynn, J.R. (1991). *Asian Americans: Achievement beyond IQ.* Hillsdale, NJ: Lawrence Erlbaum Associates Inc.

Garber, J., Braafledt, N., & Zeman, J. (1991). The regulation of sad effect: An information-processing perspective. In J. Garber & K.A. Dodge (Eds.), *The development of emotion.* Cambridge: Cambridge University Press.

Gates, A.I. (1917). Recitation as a factor in memorizing. *Archives of Psychology, 6,* No. 40.

Gelman, R. (1978). Cognitive development. *Annual Review of Psychology, 29,* 297–332.

Gesell, A., & Thompson, H. (1929). Learning and growth in identical infant twins: An experimental study by the method of co-twin control. *Genetic Psychology Monographs, 6,* 1–124.

Glass, D.C., & Singer, J.E. (1972). *Urban stress: Experiments on noise and social stressors.* New York: Academic Press.

Hart, B., & Risley, T. (1995). *Meaningful differences in everyday parenting and intellectual development in young American children.* Baltimore: Brookes.

Hayes, J.R. (1981). *The complete problem solver.* Philadelphia: Franklin Institute Press.

Hayes, J.R. & Flower, L.S. (1986). Writing research and the writer. *American Psychologist, 41,* 1106–1113.

Herrnstein, R J., & Murray, C. (1994). *The bell curve: Intelligence and class structure in American life.* New York: Free Press.

Holt, J. (1964). *How children fail.* New York: Pitman.

Howe, M.J.A. (1985). *A teacher's guide to the psychology of learning.* Oxford: Blackwell.

Howe, M.J.A. (1989) *Fragments of genius: The strange feats of idiots savants.* London: Routledge.

Howe, M.J.A. (1990). *The origins of exceptional abilities*. Oxford: Blackwell.

Howe, M.J.A. (1997). *IQ in question: The truth about intelligence*. London: Sage.

Howe, M.J.A., Davidson, J.W., Moore, D.G., & Sloboda, J.A. (1995). Are there early childhood signs of musical ability? *Psychology of Music, 23*, 162–176.

Howe, M.J.A., Davidson, J.W., & Sloboda, J.A. (in press). Innate talents: reality or myth? *Behavioral and Brain Sciences*.

Howe, M.J.A. & Griffey, H. (1995). *Give your child a better start: How to encourage early learning*. London: Penguin.

Howe, M.J.A. & Smith, J. (1988). Calendar calculating in "idiots savants": How do they do it? *British Journal of Psychology, 79*, 371–386.

Kolb, B. (1965). Achievement motivation training in underachieving high-school boys. *Journal of Personality and Social Psychology, 2*, 783–792.

Lave, J. (1977).Tailor-made experiments and evaluating the intellectual consequences of apprenticeship training. *The Quarterly Newsletter of the Institute for Comparative Human Development, 1*, 1–3.

Lepper, M.R., Green, D., & Nisbett, R.E. (1973). Undermining children's intrinsic interest with extrinsic reward: A test of the overjustification hypothesis. *Journal of Personality and Social Psychology, 9*, 260–265.

McClelland, D.C. (1978). Managing motivation to expand human freedom. *American Psychologist, 33*, 201–210.

McGraw, M. (1935). *Growth: A study of Johnny and Jimmy*. New York: Appleton-Century-Crofts.

McGraw, M. (1939). Later development of children specially trained during infancy: Johnny and Jimmy at school age. *Child Development, 10*, 1–19.

Malpass, R.S., & Devine, G. (1981). Guided memory in eyewitness identification. *Journal of Applied Psychology, 66*, 343–350.

Matheny, K., & Edwards, C. (1974). Academic improvement through an experi-mental classroom management system. *Journal of School Psychology, 12*, 222–232.

Meadows, S. (1993). *The child as a thinker*. London: Routledge.

Meadows, S. (1996). *Parenting behaviour and children's cognitive development*. Hove, UK: Psychology Press.

Nelson, K., Carskaddon, G., & Bonvillian, J.D. (1973). Syntax acquisition: Impact of experimental variation in adult verbal interaction with the child. *Child Development, 44*,497–504.

Northedge, A. (1990). *The good study guide*. Milton Keynes, UK: Open University.

Raugh, M.R., & Atkinson, R.C. (1975). A mnemonic method for learning a second language vocabulary. *Journal of Educational Psychology, 67*, 1–16.

Schenk, E. (1960). *Mozart and his times*. (Edited and translated from the German by R. and C. Winston.) London: Secker & Warburg.

Schliemann, A. (1988). Understanding the combinatorial system: Development, school learning, and everyday experience. *The Quarterly Newsletter of the Institute for Comparative Human Development, 10*, 3–7.

Schmidt, W.H.O. (1966). Socio-economic status, schooling, intelligence, and scholastic progress in a community in which education is not yet compulsory. *Paedogica Europa, 2*, 275–286.

Scribner, S. (1984). Studying working intelligence. In B. Rogoff & J. Lave (Eds.), *Everyday cognition: Its development in social context*. Cambridge, MA: Harvard University Press.

Seligman, M.A.P. (1975). *Helplessness: On depression, development and death*. San Francisco: Freeman.

Sloboda, J.A. (1985). *The musical mind: The cognitive psychology of music*. London: Oxford University Press.

Sloboda, J.A., Davidson, J.W., & Howe, M.J.A. (1994). Is everyone musical? *The Psychologist, 7*, 349–354.

Sloboda, J.A., Davidson, J.W., Howe, M.J.A., & Moore, D.G. (1996). The role of practice in the development of performing musicians. *British Journal of Psychology, 87*, 399–412.

Sloboda, J.A., & Howe, M.J.A. (1991). Biographical precursors of musical excellence: An interview study. *Psychology of Music, 19*, 3–21.

Smith, S.M. (1979). Remembering in and out of context. *Journal of Experimental Psychology: Human Learning and Memory, 5*, 460–471.

Sosniak, L.A. (1985) Learning to be a concert pianist. In B.S. Bloom (Ed.), *Developing talent in young people*. New York: Ballantine.

Stevenson, H.W., & Stigler, J.W. (1993). *The learning gap*. New York: Summit.

Super, C. (1976) Environmental effects on motor development: The case of "African infant precocity". *Developmental Medicine and Child Neurology, 18*, 561–567.

Turnure, J., Buium, N., & Thurlow, M. (1976). The effectiveness of interrogatives for promoting verbal elaboration productivity in young children. *Child Development, 11*, 780–787.

Wang, M. & Stiles, B. (1976). An investigation of children's concepts of self-responsibility for their school learning. *American Educational Research Journal, 13*, 159–179.

Wasik, B.H., Ramey, C.T., Bryant, D.M., & Sparling, J.J. (1990). A longitudinal study of two early intervention strategies: Project CARE. *Child Development, 61*, 1682–1696.

Weisberg, R.W. (1993). *Creativity: Beyond the myth of genius*. New York: Freeman.

Westfall, R.S. (1980). Newton's marvelous years of discovery and their aftermath: Myth versus manuscript. *Isis, 71*, (No. 256) 109–121.

Whitehurst, G.J., Falco, F.L., Lonigan, C.J., Fischel, J.E., DeBaryshe, B.D., & Valdez-Menchaca, M.C. (1988). Accelerating language development through picture book reading. *Developmental Psychology, 24*, 552–559.

Wiener, N. (1953). *Ex-prodigy: My childhood and youth*. New York: Simon & Schuster.

Wynn, K. (1992). Addition and subtraction by human infants. *Nature, 358*, 749–750.

Zigler, E., & Seitz, V. (1982). Social policy and intelligence. In R.J. Sternberg (Ed.), *Handbook of human intelligence*. New York: Cambridge University Press.

Author index

Subject index

gambling skills and IQ, 67–68
genetic causation, 150
genius, 123, 149
    causes of, 124
    instances of, 123
giftedness, *see* innate gifts
gymnastic skills, 42–43

habituation, 23, 149
Head Start, 46–49, 149
    criticisms of, 47, 69
home and school learning environments, 50
hothouse regime, 45, 149
How children fail, 73

imitative learning, 24, 149
improving writing skills, 141–145
    by revising when writing, 142
    sentences in writing, 143
impulsivity, 74, 78
incentives, 151
independence of abilities, 61–64
infant learning, 21–24
innate gifts and talents, 115–120, 151
instinctive behaviour, 21, 151
intelligence and specific abilities, 65–68
intrinsic motivation, 79–82, 151
IQ (Intelligence Quotient), 151
IQ and high abilities, 114–115
IQ contrasted with practical skills, 67–68, 115
IQ gains, 68–70
IQ scores, 30, 47, 49, 66, 151
    and adoption, 69
    and intervention programmes, 69
    and schooling, 69–70
    improvements in, 68–70
    in immigrants, 115
    stability of, 68
IQ tests as predictors of competence, 66

Japanese schools, 78

keyword method and foreign language words,
    105–106, 151
knowledge, as sistinct from skills, 4, 8

language, benefits of, 109, 25, 31–32

language, exposure to, 49
language acceleration, 27–32
    benefits of 31–32
language learning, 25–32
language-related parental activities, 28–32
learned helplessness, 88–90, 151
    causes of, 89
learning difficulties in students, 127–130
learning for its own sake, 80
learning principles, 6–18, 101–108
learning strategies, 102–108
link-making and learning, 14
list learning, 13–14
locus of control, 75, 84–88, 151
    and school achievement, 86
    perceptions of, 87–88
    strengthening of, 85, 86–87
look and say reading approach, 36–37, 152

making meaningful connections, 11–14
mathematical expertise, 119
memory aids, 103–106, 152
memory for digit lists, 64
mental state, 58, 152
mental state and performance, 57–58
metaphors, 14, 152
mnemonics, 103–106, 152
monitoring tasks, 56–57
monitoring reading progress, 139
mood, 58
motivation, 7, 73–99, 111–114
    varieties of, 79–99
    and high achievements, 111–114
Mozart, Wolfgang Amadeus, 112, 117
musical practising, 108, 119
musical performing skills, 48, 117–119

newborn babies, 21
Newton, Isaac, 112
note taking, 106–107, 152
numeracy, 37–40, 152

odours and habituation, 23–24
operant conditioning, 23, 152
organising learning activities, 130–134

parental encouragement, 25–45
Pavlov, Ivan, 23

UNIVERSITY OF WOLVERHAMPTON
LEARNING RESOURCES